Travis C
Sheriff's Office,
1976-2002

By Tommy Blackwell

Inquiries should be addressed to

Publisher name

Address

City, state zip

www.website.com

First edition

First printing

Although information herein is based on the author's extensive experience and knowledge, it is not intended to substitute for the services of qualified professionals

Printed in the United States of America

At XXX Printing in Austin, Texas

Dedication

The movies and television make you think the best cops work for the FBI, the CIA, or the NSA or are on a SEAL team.

Those agencies are sexy and glamorous. I have met many of those cops and they are all good cops. But, you should know that many of the best cops in the world work in your community.

They are working in the traffic detail, in investigations, in the jail, at the training academy, or in other specialized units.

These men and women choose not to join those glamorous agencies but to stay in their chosen city, town or county. Maybe it's a family thing, maybe it's the way he or she feels about the neighborhood. Whatever the reason, they are super cops, capable of incredible feats of courage, strength, and compassion, while living right next door.

I have had the pleasure and good fortune to work with and for many of these folks. They have enriched my life with their unselfish donation of their time, their hearts, and, in some cases, their lives.

My experience has been in the Travis County Sheriff's Office in Texas, which includes Austin, the Capitol of Texas, and much of the surrounding area. Many of them still work at the Travis County Sheriff's Office today. Some work at other agencies in and surrounding Austin.

Cops don't have total control because a suspect always has a choice and may or may not follow instructions. The suspect always has a choice and may or may not obey commands or follow instructions. These officers willingly walk in the shadows of Heaven and Hell. It will be Heaven if everything turns out okay, but it can be absolute Hell if it goes the other way.

They give me peace to know that day after day, they are there, whether you appreciate them or not, whether you ever need them or not. They go to work to keep you and me safe.

Thanks, guys, I know you are there, and I appreciate it every day.

This book is based on my personal experiences. It spans more than twenty-five years, and all the incidents are true.

Table of Contents

Chapter One

Chaos Among the Ruins

It was 11:30 pm on a dark moonless night; I was standing in an auto junkyard when I heard the first loud "thunk" of a big fat raindrop on the metal roof of the car next to me.

I had been called by the radio dispatcher to investigate a disturbance at this junkyard. I was twenty-two years old and on patrol for the Travis County Sheriff's Office. It was quiet, except for the sound of rain.

I heard another raindrop. I looked at the sky and saw only stars; it didn't look like rain. There were no clouds. I heard another "thunk." And another. It was only then that I realized that after each "raindrop" I had also heard a soft low "bang" two hundred and fifty, maybe three hundred yards away on the hill overlooking the junkyard.

It finally dawned on me! That is not rain! I snapped into action.

I shut off my department-issue flashlight, slid behind a large car, and crouched down.

Someone was shooting at me! They were using the beam from my flashlight to locate and aim at me.

I had been a sitting duck!

My heart pounded at one hundred and twenty beats a minute while my mind raced with what facts I had at hand.

I couldn't see anyone, I didn't hear any voices.

Was I protected behind this junked car?

Who was the shooter? Was there more than one? What type of weapon were they using? What was its effective range?

First things first.

First, I had to get out of this mess.

I crouched behind the rusting car and heard another "thud," then a half second later, "bang." That thud seemed to come from the opposite side of the car I was behind.

Had the shooter (shooters?) seen me take refuge behind this car?

I felt very vulnerable, out there, all alone, no backup and none on the way. It was only me that could get me out of this situation.

This was Texas in 1977, and the saying "One riot, One Ranger" was taken seriously. It was based around the reputation of the State of Texas investigative law enforcement agency, the legendary Texas Rangers. It meant that no matter how bad the situation, you needed only one cop to take care of it. The one riot, one ranger idea applied to all cops, and those of us in the Sheriff's office were no exception. This was the state capital. And we were the law enforcement agency that was here to do the job in the unincorporated parts of Central Texas. And as Texas police officers, we were tough with a capital "T." You didn't call for backup unless it was really bad.

We were spread out over nine hundred square miles, with maybe four deputies on duty, usually only three. Even if my handheld radio did work (which was highly unlikely) and I called for backup, it would be forty-five minutes to an hour before another deputy would arrive. By that time, it would all be over, one way or another.

I was now faced with the possibility of my death.

Over the next 25 years, I would be exposed many times to dangers and horrors, such as standing on the fields of death at Mount Carmel. I would make life-and-death decisions in a fraction of a second. My life and other's lives would hang on a single movement or a single thought. In less than a heartbeat, it would turn out good or bad. That outcome often was dependent on a single act such as the movement of the suspect's hands.

I had a lot to learn.

But I didn't have to learn about being shot at.

Having experienced being shot at before, I knew the sound of the angry bee when a spiraling supersonic bullet passed close enough that you could hear the "buzz." I was familiar with the fact that I would feel the impact before I heard the report from the gun barrel.

I had grown up in the country and we shot guns. I enjoyed long hikes through our vast "backyard" (that later became part of the "Wild Basin Preserve" in western Travis County). Our house overlooked a large valley that eventually drained into Bee Creek. The hills of our valley were studded with the various trees of the area. Ashe junipers, Spanish Oak, Live Oak and an occasional Madrone. Climbing those trees, hiking the hills and swimming in the small and shallow ponds had made up much of my childhood. On more than one occasion, I had come home only to be pinned down below the twenty-five-yard gun range behind our house where my sister loved to shoot tin cans.

She was an excellent shot and loved her .22 rifle and semi-automatic pistol.

I could tell which gun she was shooting by the number of shots fired before a long pause of her reloading. If it was eleven shots, it was the rifle. If it was nine shots, it was the pistol.

I would have to wait, count her shots, and measure the quiet moments when she wasn't shooting. I might wait through several rounds of firing and reloading to be sure. Only when I was absolutely sure which weapon she was shooting, and therefore exactly when she would be reloading, would I be able to scramble up the steep hill to the safety of the house. During all this waiting and counting, I had become familiar with the sounds of supersonic bullets.

Here in the junkyard, I thought back, how many shots had I heard? Four? It was five, I recalled. Colt makes a five-shot revolver; Smith & Wesson makes a six-shot. Great. They might be reloading right now, or might be waiting for me to make a sound or movement so they could get a better aim at me.

I waited.

I waited for perhaps thirty minutes. While I waited, I had plenty of time to think about what had happened.

The sheriff's radio dispatcher would have received a telephone call reporting a disturbance in this junkyard. I had been dispatched and arrived. I radioed that I was on the scene and began to walk around and see if I could find someone. I had shone my flashlight all over the area. I was so naive about light control that I had probably stood in my own headlights, making me an easy target and reducing my night vision to a small illuminated area.

I walked into the driveway of the junkyard and made myself as obvious as I could. About three hundred yards away was another street that housed two notorious brothers.

The Tanzetti brothers -- Ricky and Jimmy. Ages seventeen and nineteen, they lived in a small two-bedroom shack with their mother. They had been in trouble with cops for years. They had one car that they tried to hop up, but it was just a junker Plymouth with bad exhaust. They drank alcohol and took drugs. They were suspected of dealing drugs, too, and they were always ready to fight at any time, any place.

The Tanzettis would be just like them to call in a bogus call and then take potshots at the deputy who showed up.

I was angry.

My night vision had improved greatly since I had turned off my light. I could now make out the lights of the houses on the street where the Tanzettis lived. I was sure that I could see the Tanzettis' house.

I decided they had gotten bored or lost interest after I cut off my light. Still, I kept carefully inside the deep shadows of junked cars, the tin fence, and the tall shrubs as I made my way back to my patrol car.

Once in my car, I was careful not to place my foot on the brake pedal, as this would turn on the brake lights. I stepped on the parking brake, started the engine, put the car in drive and released the brake.

I drove with my lights off down the block and around the corner. Once around the corner and out of sight, I switched on the lights and drove straight to their house.

It was on Braker Lane, right across from the local Seven-Eleven. The front of the house was illuminated by the store lights from across the street. The gravel driveway announced my arrival as my patrol car crunched to a stop. It was okay with me; I wanted them to know I was there. The lights of the old simple house are on, and their Plymouth is in the driveway. I knocked on the door. No answer. I knocked and stated "Sheriff's Office." No answer. I consider my options. I have no proof it was these guys.

We do not have 9-1-1 and telephone calls are not recorded. There is no automatic feed of name, address and number as is now standard with 9-1-1 calls. There would be no record of the call.

I knocked again, real loud and yelled "Sheriff's Office!"

I have no legal authority to enter, even though I am certain they are in there. And if they are, they are refusing to answer the door; they are hiding from me for some reason. And I am certain I know what that reason is. It was the Tanzettis who were shooting at me. And now that I am here to confront and question them, they do not have the balls to talk to me.

Fine.

I would leave and think about it. It was a very frustrating situation. I felt as if I had been led into a trap and then intentionally used for target practice. I had no evidence, no witnesses and little hope of obtaining any.

Later when I talked it over with senior officers, they offered little solid advice to act on.

The new sheriff had changed many procedures, but most of the old timers were still there and they were as ineffective as ever.

They suggested that I would have to wait to "get them."

Less than a month later at a beer joint just inside the city limits, the older Tanzetti brother, Jimmy, had gotten into an argument over a woman. The argument ended up in the parking lot, where Jimmy was beaten within inches of his life with a pool stick. His attacker finished the beating by stomping and jumping on Jimmy after he was unconscious in the gravel parking lot. He was in the hospital for three weeks, being treated for a broken jaw, nose, both arms, fingers and hips and legs, not to mention missing teeth.

He came home from the hospital in a wheelchair, a changed man. It was another year before he would walk with the help of crutches. It was during that time that the younger brother moved away. We never had any further calls about the Tanzettis. I never learned what happened to Jimmy's assailant. It didn't matter. I didn't know if it was karma or what, but it reinforced my belief that I didn't have to waste time or energy worrying about how to "get" someone.

I had begun with the Travis County Sheriff's Office in the fall of 1976. Sheriff Raymond Frank had begun his second four-year term in January that year.

He had come into office a retired Air Force colonel with CIB (Criminal Investigation Bureau) experience and military organization skills strong enough to get him elected over the "good ol boy" incumbent, T.O. Lang.

T.O. Lang had been the stereotypical Texas sheriff. He had been in office for over sixteen years.

Big, with a big cowboy hat, mirrored sunglasses, white long-sleeved shirt tucked in over a large belly, with a star pinned to the left breast pocket. T. O. was a friend to all the right people and an ass kicker to anyone whom he thought was criminal. By 1972 he was not what the liberal democrats of Travis County wanted as their sheriff. I was in total agreement with them.

Raymond Frank came into the office and changed things quickly.

He required reports to be written of all crimes investigated. A no-brainer but this had not been done in the past. He had clerical staff read and then record each name mentioned in an offense report on a three-by-five card and filed alphabetically for future reference and cross-referencing by investigators. He staffed the warrants section to organize and track the warrants that the county and felony district courts issued.

He created the Investigations Division and assigned senior officers to investigate crimes, make arrests, and obtain warrants for the arrest of suspected criminals.

He helped obtain federal funding to build a "radio room" in the middle of the offices of the sheriff's portion of the courthouse. (However, it would be years before we had decent radio coverage.) At least we now had three FCC-licensed frequencies and real radio room equipment.

All of this was new and innovative for the sleepy town of Austin and the sleepy sheriff's office that performed law enforcement for perhaps ten thousand citizens who then lived in the unincorporated parts of Travis County.

Ah, Travis County, the Heart of Texas, is home to Austin, the capital, also, home to Pflugerville, a quiet German community northeast of Austin, West Lake Hills, and Rollingwood, residential cities just west of Austin. Manor, a historic black community east of Austin; Lakeway, a relatively new retirement community out west and fifteen other small but peaceful cities.

We had rolling hills covered with live oak and Ashe juniper trees (incorrectly known as cedar trees). We had armadillos and horned toads. We had rivers and lakes and creeks and streams. We had Willie Nelson, who had just had his third annual Fourth of July picnic and was on his way to stardom. We had beer joints and dance halls that sponsored Nickel Beer Night every Wednesday. We had green belt parks that enveloped miles of local creeks and streams and three beautiful lakes perfect for water skiing and fishing. There was the University of Texas that brought us culture and liberal students, who liked the recreation and beauty of the area, found employment, and stayed after they finished school. We had Bergstrom Air Force Base, which for a time was the number two requested "last tour of duty" for retiring Air Force officers, second only to Panama. We had sweet quiet two-lane roads, turning and twisting over the hills and through the countryside. Hardly any traffic to worry about.

This is where I grew up; these were the roads that I learned to drive on. This was my community and I belonged here.

I had joined the Sheriff's Office with disdain in my heart for the overweight stupid white bigots that so many Texas law enforcement officers were in the sixties and seventies.

I had my share of encounters with these sorts while growing up, obvious "control freaks" who couldn't hold any other job. Telling my friends that I suspected the police may have been paid by the pound. I made mean jokes about their weight.

They made me determined that a law enforcement officer could be reasonable, fair, intelligent and capable of arresting large angry people. I was determined to be the police officer that I thought all cops should be.

I just wanted to do the right thing and I would have plenty of opportunities to do that.

A few months before the junkyard incident, I had been called to a disturbance at a house in a Hispanic community. I arrived and could see a large gathering in the backyard, it looked peaceful, just a big picnic. A smoking barbecue pit, music, lots of people.

The patriarch of the house, Mr. Jorge Ramos, met me at the front door. He explained that it was his son's twenty-first birthday party. All his friends and family were here and because it was Jorge Junior's twenty-first birthday, he was allowed to drink all the beer he wanted.

Only problem was that the son was now rip-roaring, fighting drunk.

He would slug it out with anyone. His father's words were sincere and concerned. He also had a large reddish-purple spot above his left eye. I could see how sincere he was.

I knew that normally, these quiet, community-minded folks avoided any contact with law enforcement. While they were the true natives of this land, they were treated with disrespect by many police. Sometimes they were accused of being illegal aliens, threatened with arrest and deportation to Mexico, or just called names like "dumb spick." I had overheard other officers talking about the difficulties in dealing with people whose language they did not understand. "Mexicans are like cue balls," is what I had heard, "The harder you hit them, the more English you get out of them."

I kept my opinions to myself. In the squad room, I was outnumbered. The bigots ruled.

But here, in this man's house, he was asking me for help.

As we were sitting in his living room, I asked him what he wanted me to do.

"Can you take him to jail? That way he could sleep off the drunk and not hurt anyone else?"

His mom and a few other relatives were in the room. They all nodded and murmured agreement.

It seems that for over two hours, they had "corralled" this healthy wild drunk twenty-one-year-old with a human wall of thirty to forty friends and that they were wearing out. They were standing in a giant circle in the backyard with the son in the center.

Periodically, Jorge Jr. would decide who would get the next beating and charge that poor person and the fight would be on. The rest of the circle would come to the defense of the selected "victim," drag the kicking and cussing youngster back into the center of the circle, until he was released, and it was like trying to hold a wild animal, his father explained. They were desperately keeping him pinned into this backyard so that he would not hurt others or cause large-scale damage. But they were wearing down, and he was not.

They needed help, so they had called the sheriff.

His father asked if I could arrest the boy on a minor charge so that he would spend the night in jail, then be released the next day and not have a long, complicated criminal justice proceeding. All they wanted was some help. Some help that I believed I could offer.

As a Texas peace office, I had the authority to make arrests without a warrant for any criminal offense committed within my presence. From what they had told me, I would walk out the back door and see the son committing one of several crimes, assault being the primary possibility.

They wanted me to arrest him but not to hurt him. "You will not use the club?" the father asked.

He was referring to the nightstick, twenty-four inches of hard black plastic that I carried on my left hip.

"No problem." I took the club out of its holding ring and placed it between the cushions of the sofa.

It really was no problem for me. I had received no training in the use of the nightstick, so not using it would be easier than using it, actually.

We made a quick, rough plan. While the group had the boy surrounded, we would approach from outside the circle. I would enter the circle, place handcuffs on him and then take him to jail. If I needed help, they would be there.

Only years later would I realize just how poorly planned this action was. But at the time, it seemed right. I had the family on my side, I had my skill and strength and one drunken kid. It should be no problem.

I recall that day, the bright sun, the look of desperation on the faces of family and friends, the bloody noses and mouths of many of those in the circle and the wild look in the young man's eyes.

For a moment, I saw that he was confused and concerned about my presence. That was good. I wanted to surprise him with politeness and a gentle application of a pair of handcuffs. I smiled I approached slowly. He looked around the circle and realized he was trapped. I expected him to charge me, and so did everybody else.

Just as I was about to get within lunging distance, he bolted. Like a white-tailed deer, I thought. Really fast and unstoppable. He bowled through the circle of people and ran for the back fence -- a common three-strand barbed wire fence. The top strand of wire was three feet off the ground. He hurtled it like the wild animal he was.

I was right behind him. Not as graceful, carrying an extra fifteen pounds of leather belts, gun, extra ammunition, handcuffs and handheld radio and wearing cowboy boots. But I was determined not to lose him. I straddled the fence and started running. He ran right down the middle of the street that paralleled his parents' property. We ran for less than a half-mile and he gave out. That was good, because the only thing I had going for me in the strength area was my age. I was smoking a pack of cigarettes each day, drinking as much beer as any other cop and eating high-fat, high-speed junk food. I wasn't going to last much longer, either. It would be several years before I found fitness and health to be important issues.

He stood heaving and breathing in the road, so I told him between my breaths that he was under arrest and then placed my handcuffs on him, behind his back.

He politely complied.

We began walking back to my patrol car and his house.

I was proud of myself. Real proud.

I had done what I set out to do. I had helped citizens who had asked for help. I had done it without unnecessary force or violence. I had done it without a bullshit tough guy image. I had done it, even when it went outside of the plan. I was very pleased with myself.

I was busy congratulating myself and did not notice that my prisoner had regained his breathing, was looking around the area and was contemplating his next action.

We were about fifty feet from his backyard. All the party guests were standing around watching us walk up the street. I had his left elbow in my right hand and was walking on his left side. For him, it was easy. He stepped his right foot across in front of me, pushing his weight into me and then quickly stepping out to the right. And he was gone. Off and running again.

Hands cuffed behind his back, he headed straight for what he thought was sanctuary -- his own backyard. He went to jump the barbed wire fence again, only this time, with his hands behind his back, he didn't have the coordination and balance of the first time. One foot cleared the fence, the other did not.

He went down hard on his left shoulder and the left side of his head.

I was right behind him.

Jeez, he looked bad.

When he hit the ground, he had crumpled in a pile, and now he wasn't moving. As I reached him, so did all of the partygoers. We huddled over him. Many were saying, "Is he dead?" He looked dead. He had landed hard on that side of his head and shoulder. He could have easily broken his neck and been "DRT." (Police lingo for "Dead Right There.") I was hoping he wasn't dead.

My heart raced, because this was not what I had in mind. As I kneeled beside him, I could feel his pulse in his neck and see his chest rise and fall. He was unconscious, but alive!

I said, "He is just knocked out." I was still very concerned about a possible spinal injury. He may have been alive, but was he paralyzed? Was he in danger of further spinal injury? As I worried over my prisoner, the crowd was pressing in. I was aware of their comments and concerns; I explained that he was just unconscious, but that I was concerned about his neck and spine. I wanted EMS to respond and I wanted to prevent any chance of further injury.

As he was lying partially on his side, I began removing the handcuffs, as I knew that EMS would want to place him on his back without the cuffs.

Yells from the outer fringes of the crowd came to my attention:

"He killed him and now he is taking the handcuffs off him!"

"He is removing the evidence!"

"No", I called out." He is unconscious and I am making him comfortable."

Other partygoers closer to me assured the outer group this was true.

"I am calling for EMS." I held up my handheld radio.

It was only then that I realized the radio dispatcher was calling me. "Unit 204! Unit 204 do you copy? Unit 204 this is Travis County, do you copy?"

Relieved that the radio even worked, I replied that I could hear them and the dispatcher immediately shot back, "Do you need backup? Neighbors have called the Austin Police Department and say that you need help. APD has called the Sheriff's Office and wants to know if you want me to send backup."

"No!"

I didn't need gasoline thrown on this fire.

I could understand the neighbor's concern. They had been watching this situation and the last they saw was the police officer getting swarmed by the crowd and they could hear the outer crowd's angry shouts: "He killed him!"

But I knew that if other officers were dispatched, they would be told that I was in trouble in a Hispanic neighborhood and that the group had me pinned down.

That would only incite the responding officers' bigotry and unnecessary hatred.

What was a bad situation could become worse by having angry gun-toting cops show up looking for some "Mexican butt" to kick.

"No, I do not need backup," I said, "I need EMS, but do not send any other officers."

The dispatcher didn't believe me.

She asked me again and again I said that I only wanted EMS dispatched. She finally accepted what I was saying and acknowledged that she would have medical professionals en route.

Mr. Ramos and I calmed the crowd, explaining again and again to other drunks that the son was okay and that EMS was on the way.

It turned out, he was okay.

EMS arrived and quickly understood the situation. After their evaluation of the now semiconscious young man, they agreed that he should be transported for further evaluation.

These compassionate EMTs understood that I didn't want to put this guy in jail, just get him restrained until he could sober up.

They had the perfect mechanism for it.

They used cloth straps called "soft restraints" to tie his wrists and ankles to the steel bars of the collapsible gurney.

No matter how he struggled, he could not get free.

They explained to the group that he needed X-rays and was going to be transported to the hospital. I knew and they knew that he would be restrained until he was very polite and cooperative with the hospital staff. That would take hours. He would sleep off most of the drunk. Later, after being examined, he would be released.

I explained the "new" plan to the father and he understood and agreed that it was acceptable.

The youngster was transported and released later that evening and no charges were filed. Everything turned out just fine.

Except, I learned that it wasn't always easy to make things come out right.

So many people were ready to jump to the use of force and violence.

When the son became violent, the group had tried to use violence to restrain him. That didn't work.

When the group thought that I had killed him, they were ready to kick my ass.

When the neighbors thought I was getting my ass kicked, they wanted more cops to come and do more ass kicking.

I was proud but humbled. It was not easy to be the sort of cop I wanted to be.

Chapter Two

Welcome to Texas: A Day of Chaos and Cluck

Every person who becomes a police officer wants to be involved in dangerous situations. They may have different reasons for that desire, but we all want to be in a critically difficult situation and survive it with honor. So when we are at work, we are ready for that situation to occur. We don't care what form it takes, just bring it on. However, sometimes, an obviously dangerous situation turns out to be something entirely different from what was expected.

Back in those early days, weekend day shifts were mostly boring affairs. Very little to do, besides drive by people's homes that were on vacation. Drink coffee. Eat lunch. Hope for a call. Sitting at the intersection of Braker Lane and IH 35 one Sunday day shift, I was just wishing there was something to do.

The radio dispatcher called and told me that the state highway patrol helicopter (DPS unit 100) was calling for any Travis County unit in the area of Highway 290 and US 183. That was only four or five miles from where I was!

I changed the radio channel, told the helicopter my radio identifier and asked what I could do to help.

They quickly told me that they were in pursuit of a stolen vehicle coming towards Austin and they had no ground cars involved in the pursuit!

Oh, yeah! This would make my day! I radioed that I would be en route, hit my lights and sirens and hauled butt onto the expressway!

I loved my patrol car. It was a 1976 Chevrolet four-door Nova. Looked like an ugly box, but had a big roaring V8, topped by an excellent intake and exhaust system. It ran like a spotted ass ape. The front end and steering were so good that I had confided in another deputy that the car drove at one hundred miles per hour just as good in the grassy center median as it did on the pavement. He said he drove it in the ditch, too. I believed him.

As I headed for the intercept point, the state troopers in the helicopter told me a bit more of the story. A man had been involved in a high-speed pursuit about an hour east of Austin, including running through a roadblock that had flattened his tires. The suspect then fled on foot through the woods and the local cops called for the helicopter. That was about two hours ago, but ten minutes ago, two old folks living on a nearby farm got free from their bindings to say the suspect had broken into their house, tied them up and stolen their vehicle. He had also stolen a handgun.

They described their car as a yellow VW van with black bumpers. They couldn't remember their license plate but were in the process of looking it up when the helicopter spotted the van just outside of Austin headed my way.

Woooo Haaa! Here I came. As I was blasting along the divided highway, I was watching the sky to see the approaching helicopter. It was a busy Sunday afternoon and traffic was unusually heavy. Maybe there was a football game in town. Soon, I saw the chopper, and I knew my target was getting close. I was in the left lane and had slowed to twenty to thirty miles per hour, lights and sirens still blaring, traffic behind me stacking up, traffic beside me slowing down, and I was watching for the distinctive yellow Volkswagen van with black bumpers. Sure enough, about two hundred yards in front of the helicopter was the van coming right at me in the opposite lanes. I let it pass, and then I dove the Nova into the center ditch and jumped it out like the rocket sled it was, landing just a few feet behind the VW. Dirt and grass were everywhere. Traffic was screeching to a halt on both roadways.

I tailed in on the van and the van driver pulled over. Now, all traffic was at a dead stop in both directions.

I snapped off my siren.

It was still deafening outside.

The helicopter hovered about fifty feet up and thirty feet off to my right.

Using my car for cover, I opened my door, took out my pistol, pointed it at the driver, who was looking at me in his outside mirror and motioned with my left hand for him to come toward me.

The helicopter overhead was roaring. The grass was being blown flat on both sides of the road. The smell of burnt rubber was heavy in the air.

My heart was pounding. I was effecting the felony traffic stop, ready for anything, as the driver began his exit from the car. Not only did he get out, but so did a female passenger.

They walked partway back toward me and I came from behind my door to motion for them to place their hands on the side of the van. (Another stupid tactic taught to cops back then; only later would we realize how stupid.)

I approached and began a frisk of both subjects for weapons.

Terry vs. Ohio, a famous 1968 Supreme Court case, gives peace officers the authority to do such searches when a reasonably prudent man would have been warranted in believing the suspect was armed and thus presented a threat to the officer's safety while he was investigating the suspicious behavior. It didn't say anything about females. I wasn't taking any chances. She got frisked, just like the man.

At that time my dispatcher was calling me on the radio. Repeatedly. Telling me to go to the inner-city frequency to talk with the helicopter.

Not now, guys, I was busy. Couldn't they see I had two people at gunpoint?

At the time, I carried only one pair of handcuffs (another lesson that I would have to learn later) so I cuffed the two to each other and escorted them at gunpoint back toward my car.

The helicopter flew away. I was puzzled, but thought maybe they were concerned about the huge traffic jam that we were creating and decided that I had everything under control.

Whatever the case, I had the suspects and put them in my back seat. I quickly checked the van to see that it had no more occupants, and then got behind the wheel of my car.

The radio was crackling, "DPS 100 to Travis County unit 204, DPS 100 to Travis County unit 204"

"Go ahead," I said.

"The suspect we are looking for is a black male, repeat black male, do you copy?"

Well Holy Jamollies! Yeah, I copied! The two folks in my back seat may have been a little tanned, but they were definitely white people.

As it turned out, it was the new golf pro and his wife driving from Florida to take a job in Lago Vista, a beautiful golfing community on Lake Travis northwest of Austin.

After I explained the whole story, they admitted that there were not that many yellow VW vans with black bumpers on the road. After they understood the situation and were visibly relaxed, I was able to say, with a straight face:

"Welcome to Texas."

And then, sometimes dangerous situations are everything you could ever imagine, and more.

Part of my patrol district was in a six-block area that for years the city of Austin had avoided annexing. Complete with run-down mobile homes, beat-up frame houses, leaky septic systems, farm animals and citizens who referred to their neighborhood by its street name, "Rat Flats." The streets had potholes and the dogs were all dangerous. The children grew up hard and mean.

One such child was Morris Dale Wilson. The oldest of five barefoot kids, Morris Dale had drunken parents who had beaten him every single day of his adolescent life. Morris Dale had a bad reputation by 1976, and I was told that if I ever had to arrest him, I should tell him it was for anything but public intoxication.

Public intoxication -- a low-level misdemeanor crime that was an important tool in any peace officer's bag of tricks. A person commits an offense if the person appears in a public place while intoxicated to the degree that the person may endanger the person or another.

When committed in the presence of a peace officer, PI was a warrantless arrest offense.

Say a cop gets a call from a beer joint about a disturbance, then arrives and sees an angry confrontation between two patrons. Bingo, a simple arrest for public intoxication, takes care of the problem. No waiting until someone gets assaulted or something gets broken.

However, young Morris Dale had been arrested so many times for public intoxication by his eighteenth birthday that he found the idea very offensive and he'd fight it every time.

And it would be a fight. At six foot three inches, two hundred pounds and no fat, Morris Dale was lean and tough, a street fighter since childhood.

Sure enough, that radio call came in. A pleasant fall Sunday and the Hi Ho Inn reported an unknown subject kicking the wall outside. The Hi Ho was a sleezy beer joint often referred as a "dive" located on the far end of North Lamar Blvd. Nothing but derelicts drank there. I can smell it even now as I write the words. It stank like a combination of old spilled beer, stale cigarette smoke and a redneck's armpit. I began heading that way. I was not the primary officer. My adjoining district officer, Bob Vann had been assigned the call, and I was rolling his way, just in case he asked me to assist. Before either of us arrived, another call was broadcast. A few blocks away, in Rat Flats, a caller said that two men had just tried to tear the door of her mobile home. She gave a brief description. Bob radioed back that the description fit Morris Dale and his running buddy Junior Gomez. He also said that I should be headed his way, as they were always trouble.

I liked Bob. He was a big guy who really cared if he did police work the right way versus the easy way. He had genuine ethics and I looked up to him. Everybody called him Vann.

When he radioed that he had located the suspects and he wanted me to respond, I was less than a block away. I pulled up and jumped out of my car, making the rookie mistake of not radioing that I had arrived at Vann's location.

Vann had both subjects stopped and was talking to them against an eight-foot chain-link fence.

When he saw me approach, he turned to his detainees and said, "Y'all turn around and put your hands behind your back." They did as they were told. Vann took out his handcuffs and placed one on Morris Dale's right wrist. Morris Dale craned his head around his neck and asked, "What chall arresting me for?"

Vann did the right thing, not the easy thing.

He could have extended the truth and claimed that he was arresting Morris Dale on damage to the side of the Hi Ho. How would you ever know? It was such a dump, a few kick marks would be undetectable. He could say that Morris Dale was being arrested for the damage to the second caller's mobile home, but Vann knew the residents of Rat Flats were not model citizens and would not want to drive downtown to file charges, much less show up for hearings and trials.

Hell, he could have lied and told Morris Dale that we had warrants for armed robbery. But he didn't.

Vann told the truth.

"Public intoxication" he said, loud and clear.

I looked at him with astonishment. Before I could say a word, Morris Dale took his hands from behind his back and began climbing the eight-foot chain-link fence.

Vann grabbed his right leg that by now was chest high going up the fence. I grabbed the left. Morris kept climbing. Pulling me and Vann up as he went. Morris got to the top of the fence with a chicken coop on the opposite side.

He got a good grip on something and pulled. I couldn't believe it! Certainly, I was no heavyweight, both Vann and I combined had to weigh over three hundred pounds. He was pulling us up and over the fence, and soon all three of us were on top of the flimsy chicken coop.

Considering we were in Rat Flats it wasn't a surprise that the chicken coop wasn't built according to city code. The roof couldn't take the weight of all of us and it collapsed before any one of us could get situated.

We fell in a pile, with chickens squawking, feathers flying and people in a pile of chicken poop.

As I stood up, so did Morris. I was face to face with him, and he still had the handcuffs dangling from one wrist. I took both his wrists in my hands, looked him in the eye and said, "Morris Dale, this is not a big thing, it is just a misdemeanor arrest." He hit me on the chin with an uppercut that I never saw coming.

When I came back to consciousness, I was lying on my face in chicken poop, dimly aware that my friend and mentor was in a battle. I struggled to my feet. Morris pushed Vann away and Vann stumbled backwards over some barnyard obstacle and fell.

I again confronted Morris.

This time, I didn't try to make physical contact. I was going to sincerely get him to see the simplicity and logic of the situation. There was no need to fight.

He looked right at me as I spoke. I was telling him how this was no big deal, how a man like himself could easily handle these charges.

It was making sense to me, but I noticed that Morris was growing taller, and for some reason the sky was getting an unusual shade of red.

It was then that I became aware of Morris's friend, Junior Gomez. Little scrawny Junior was standing behind me, swinging a two-by-four like a baseball bat again and again against my lower back. Right across my kidneys. How many home runs had Junior hit? I didn't know. I just knew that Morris grew very tall as I sank into the ground. Again, I was unconscious.

I don't know for how long, maybe a few minutes, but when I awoke, the fight had moved from the chicken yard around the house and into the front yard. I was vaguely aware that Vann was talking into his handheld radio. Later I learned that he had called for help and was directing the responding Austin Police Department units to our location. My unconsciousness had made him realize this situation was serious and we needed all the reinforcements we could get. Because I had failed to call out when I had arrived, dispatch thought Vann was out there by himself and that things were really bad. They doubled his request when relaying his communications to APD. They were coming in force.

As I made my way towards them, I remember being amazed that he knew the street name and specific block that we were on. Hell, I didn't know which country I was in!

As he talked, he was struggling to place the handcuffs on Morris.

It was time for me to use strength and technique, I decided.

I came up beside Morris and tripped him with an easy back kick behind one of his knees. As he went down, I rode on top of him, knocking the breath out of him as I landed on his chest. I closed my left hand around his throat and my right hand around his testicles.

I had him now. I had an iron grip, and I could hold most peoples' arms together with one hand. I had broken several of those grip strengtheners by repeatedly squeezing and releasing them until the metal heated up and bent or the plastic popped.

I had him now. I would hold his airway closed until he passed out. I would squeeze his balls if he tried to roll away. I had him.

Out of the corner of my eye, I saw movement. A lot of movement. I looked up. Vann was flying through the air, coming directly toward us, completely prone, about three feet off the ground, talking into his radio, as he flew.

Right before impact he drew back the radio and crashed it onto Morris's head as he landed on us. The radio exploded. Parts went everywhere.

Even with my iron grip, Morris Dale spoke through his closed airway, "Ah, not in the head." As if that was unsportsmanlike. How was he able to speak with my "iron grip" closed on his throat? I wondered.

About then, I realized that I could hear sirens. The wonderful sound of responding backup. The beautiful melody of "Here comes help!" And they were coming, too. About two dozen of them. The Austin guys drove blue and white cars blowing around the corners at fifty. Tires smoking, doors popping open, guys in blue running towards the three of us rolling in a pile.

I was whipped, and when I saw the first fresh hands on Morris, I released my grip and got out of the way. Three more jumped to take my place. Four blue uniforms and Vann were now busy finishing putting the handcuffs on Morris Dale.

I looked up the street and saw two things. Another blue and-white slid to a stop and little Junior Gomez walked slowly away with his hands in his pockets, not a care in the world.

As the APD guy exited his car, Junior came even with him. I yelled, "Get that son of a bitch!" and pointed at Junior.

Too late.

The APD guy could only see the melee on the ground at my feet and Junior took my shout as a piece of good advice to start running.

The APD guy ran past me on the sidewalk as I ran toward Junior.

Junior ran down the street for just a minute, then cut down a side yard with me hot behind him. He turned left in a backyard and headed straight for the three-foot-high chain-link fence.

He jumped it by placing only his hands and feet on the top rail in a prone flyover. I knew I didn't have the juice to do that. I was wearing a bullet-resistant vest, an extra gun tucked in the straps of the vest, and a gun belt with gun, radio, handcuffs and ammunition. I was also wearing the traditional footwear of a Texas cop, cowboy boots. I wasn't going to be able to vault the fence. So I didn't slow down as I approached.

I hit the fence in a full run about the same time Junior hit the ground on the other side. My forward movement slammed the top part of my body over the fence; I stretched out my arms to grab Junior and only tore off his shirt.

It slowed him a little, so I stumbled over the fence and we began running again. The fence on the other side of the yard was coming up quickly.

Same thing. He vaults it with his hands and feet, I slam into it, running as fast as I can, trying to take advantage of the small amount of time that he slows down to get ready for the jump.

It doesn't work any better the second time. This time I only leave red marks on his sweaty back. He is up and running and I am struggling to cross another fence.

We are now running through someone's plowed half-acre garden. The soft dirt and uneven surface make running difficult. My backup gun gets jostled out of its holster inside my shirt and is now bouncing around under my shirt next to my waist. As we run, I unbutton the bottom button and get control of the 45-caliber semi-auto. Bad news, because right then

Junior looked back to see how the chase was going. His eyes got real big when he saw the gun in my hand, and then he really started running.

I couldn't believe it. He was gone. I was stopped at a six-foot-high chicken-wire fence and Junior was nowhere in sight. Dazed and tired, I thought it seemed like a magic trick. One minute we were in eye contact, the next, he was gone and I could not get past this damn fence.

I realized there had to be a hole in the fence and began looking for it. Of course there was. I found it, crawled through it and came out on the next street over. The street where this had all begun. I stood in the center of the street and saw no Junior. I looked both ways up and down the street. No Junior. I noticed that on almost every front porch or in every lawn, a resident was standing. Looking at me. The sirens and screeching tires of the responding units had gotten everyone's attention and they were trying to see what was going on. I had put my backup gun in its holster and I looked face to face to see if I could get any help. These are not the model citizens of Pleasantville, USA. They didn't help cops. The cops were the bad guys in this neighborhood. I shrugged my shoulders and held my palms up with my elbows at my side. I looked from face to face and they just looked back. Finally, one old woman pointed with her chin, down just a bit and on the right side of the road.

I jogged in that direction. Sure enough lying in the shadows on someone's porch was Junior. I was so glad to see him that I fell down on top of him and hugged him. After all that I was out of breath and could only say one word with each exhale. I said You… are… under… arrest. He just nodded his head. I think he was glad it was over, as well.

I rolled him over, put the handcuffs on him and walked him back to the large crowd of officers the next street over.

Later, while I was at the hospital being treated for a concussion and other injuries, Junior, who claimed to have injuries, would escape from the hospital. He was charged with the felonies of aggravated assault on a peace officer and escape. Since he was already on probation for burglary, a few weeks later, when he was arrested on the new warrants, his probation was revoked and he spent five years in the state prison system. I heard when he got out, but I never saw him again. Morris was luckier. This was his first felony, so after the nine months he spent waiting in the county jail for his trial, he was granted probation, given credit for the time he had spent in jail and released.

This was just the first of seven times that I would arrest Morris Dale.

It didn't slip by me that while I was unconscious, he hadn't taken my weapon or kicked me in the head. He hadn't tried to fight dirty and he had made that comment about Vann hitting him in the head with his radio. For all his faults, Morris Dale had some standards.

In the other arrests, sometimes it was a fight, sometimes it wasn't. On at least three occasions, I simply drove up to him, opened my passenger door without getting out of my car and told him to get in. Once inside, I gave him the handcuffs and he put on them on. Other times, it was a hard fight. Always clean, always by his unstated rules of engagement. I never hit him with my fists or nightstick and I learned how to avoid that uppercut. There was no kicking. He never tried to take my gun. I always used joint locks and judo takedowns to get him on the ground, and then locked him up so I could put the handcuffs on.

I never really trusted him, but one day, when he seemed sober, I had loaned him a few bucks for lunch. When he paid me back a few weeks later, I saved those dollars like they were silver certificates.

I liked Vann because he always knew what to do.

One day, we received a call of a murder that had just occurred out on RR 2222 near a place called Four Points. The caller said that some Bandidos motorcycle types had come to his house and killed his friend with a single blast from a shotgun.

Vann was the first on the scene. He said that he would secure the witness and the scene and directed me and other responding units to travel past the house on its quarter-mile-long unpaved driveway to look for the suspects.

I was the second unit to turn off the pavement and begin down the driveway. About halfway down the driveway, I decided to test the brakes, as a recent rain had left the driveway muddy. I pushed down on the brake pedal and as I suspected, nothing happened. I did not slow down even a little. I thought maybe all the mud had gummed up the tread of my tires and that I could clean out the tread and gain better traction by driving on the grass in the yard of the now-approaching house.

I steered the car into the grass and pressed on the brake. It felt like I picked up speed.

I think that scientists have been trying to create a lubricant that has the same low coefficient of friction as wet grass.

I let off the brakes and thought that I would just steer back onto the driveway, roll past the house, and come to a stop in the pasture out back.

No, I wasn't going to do that, either! The wet grass just let the front wheels turn left or right with no change in my direction. I continued my direct path for the house!

In the last few feet I was frantically twisting the wheel any direction to keep from smashing through the house.

Just as impact with the bedroom wall was imminent, the front of the car fell out from under me and the car dove into a deep hole.

It came to a stop less than eight feet from the house. My car's rear wheels were off the ground and the front end was down in a hole.

Not just any hole, the open septic tank hole.

Oh man, it stunk! And my car was stuck!

It seems the recent rains had flooded the tank, and the residents had dug it up in a futile attempt to hand pump it during the rain storm. Being defeated, they had covered the hole with a sheet of plywood and shoveled dirt back on top to keep the plywood in place.

Wasn't that called a Burmese tiger trap?

I walked around to where Vann was attending to the witness; Vann always knew what to do.

He didn't miss a beat when I told him about my car. Instead of being concerned about the car, he told me to look for tracks in the soft mud beside the house, so that I could determine the direction of travel of the murder suspects.

I did as I was told and after ten minutes, I came back and explained there were no tracks of any kind -- footprints, tire tracks, nothing.

Vann didn't say a word; he turned and slowly looked at the "witness." The young man broke into tears and confessed to shooting his lover and making up the story about the Bandidos!

Then Vann spoke into his handheld radio. He said, "This is Travis County Unit 202, I am at the homicide scene on RR 2222, there was a wrecker nearby, if that wrecker driver is listening to this frequency, please return to the scene."

Sure enough, five minutes later, we had a free tow out of the mess I was in and a murder suspect in custody.

Vann has been the elected constable of Precinct Two of Travis County. No finer or dedicated peace officer can be found anywhere.

Chapter Three

Rattles, Reflexes, and Split-Second Decisions

While we all wanted a "hot call'' anything to break the boredom was considered a good thing in those days.

I had a sergeant, Jose Castro, who liked to work with leather. He had told all of his troops that if they ever came across a nice rattlesnake, they should kill it and bring it to him, and he would make a hat band or a belt from the hide.

He brought in his Stetson cowboy hat, complete with a handmade rattlesnake hat band and we all were in awe. It was hugely handsome, very Texan and downright macho.

Some months later, I got the call.

A lady in the eastern part of the county had a rattlesnake in her driveway and wanted a deputy to come out and kill it.

Today, I would explain the snake's benefit to the environment and, therefore to us and then gently shoo it away from the house.

But back then it was part of your duty to rid the countryside of these horrible deadly vermin. Ranchers and farmers lost valuable livestock to them. Residents had to protect their children and family pets from them. You were required to eliminate as many as you could.

I arrived at the house and found the snake, coiled in the gravel driveway. Not wanting to damage the skin, I borrowed her husband's .410 shotgun, which has a small, close pattern. I walked within fifteen feet, scuffed my boot in the gravel and the snake raised its head to strike.

BAM! The .410 blew its head off. The snake fell still in the driveway. While the relieved woman danced around me in thanks, I stood amazed, as I had never seen a snake die without writhing.

One of my earliest memories is of my mother cutting the head off a copperhead with a garden hoe. The head was gone, but the snake kept moving. A lot. It even climbed a small bush. I asked Mom if it was really dead and she said it was, but the snake didn't know it yet. At the time, it was proof that snakes had supernatural powers; they were not to be trusted and they deserved death.

But there it was -- a forty-inch rattler, dead and motionless in the driveway. Upon close examination, my shot was perfect. I had shot the head clean off. It was gone. That was the explanation for the absolute stillness.

I got a paper bag from the grateful woman, put the snake in it and resumed my tour of duty. I ended my tour a few minutes early and was greeted in the squad room by Sergeant Castro. He was eager to hear the story and see if I had indeed gotten a snake for him to make into a belt.

"Yeah" I said, "I got the snake." I opened the bag and took out the carcass. It was long and big and its diamond pattern stood out boldly all the way down to its rattles. It was very handsome.

Jose looked at it with a critical eye. I knew that if there was any imperfection in the skin, he would find it. He examined the snake from top to bottom. After a few minutes, he made his declaration: "Tommy, you have a fine snake here, I can make you a very nice belt from this. There is one thing, however. As I will be working the skin with my bare hands, would you mind trimming off about three inches of the snake? There may be a small amount of venom on that part and I could prick my skin with a bone fragment and give my self a snake bite."

"No problem" I said. "I will be happy to cut that off." Not wanting to cut it in the squad room and get blood on the table or floor, I took the snake outside to the curb.

I took out my Uncle Henry pocketknife, held the snake body in my left hand against the concrete curb and began sawing off those three inches.

I had never been one to keep a knife in great shape. As far as I was concerned, a knife was a tool and I used it for all sorts of jobs -- screwdriver, pry tool, wire cutter, bottle opener, whatever. My friends had often commented on how dull my knife blades were.

No matter, it was sawing along. With great pressure I had cut about half an inch through the two-inch muscle and bone.

That was when the snake came back to life! It wrapped itself around my left arm, from my wrist to just above the elbow. The rattles were buzzing at my left ear. I had a hold of the neck and I was not letting go. I told myself there was nothing to worry about -- it was dead and this was just "reflexes." All I had to do was finish cutting off the head. Still, it was not going fast enough. Snake blood made my grip slippery, and the dull knife made the work difficult and slow.

It was taking much too long. There I was at mid-afternoon on the front steps of the Travis County courthouse, downtown Austin, Texas, in full uniform, fighting with a rattlesnake, and my only weapon was this rusty dull knife.

I heard voices and looked up to see a man and woman walking by. They were dressed nicely, probably going to court. As I turned my head to look up at them the rattles tickled my left ear. They stopped for just a second, saw exactly what was going on, their eyes widened and they hurried on without saying a word.

I knew that I had to get this job done before someone complained to the sheriff.

I sawed on, back and forth with even more pressure, and finally, the last bit was done! Relieved, I unwrapped the snake from my arm and replaced it in the bag.

I looked at my knife and made a silent vow, then closed the blade and stood up.

The bag was buzzing and jumping at my feet. A great feeling of relief spread over me. I smiled. An awful practical joke came to mind.

By now the squad room was really full. Our off-going shift of guys, the oncoming shift and the day shift admin folks would be in there. Most had heard or knew that I had gotten a rattlesnake call that day.

I couldn't resist it. I picked up the jumping and buzzing bag and walked into the squad room.

Only Jose and I knew the true condition of the snake in the bag. Everyone else assumed the worst.

Most shift changes were social events, with officers exchanging banter and crime information. Weekend plans are made and ball game scores are discussed. Not that day. When they saw me and that bag, people were only interested in one thing -- getting out of the building. The place emptied like it was on fire. Jose and I laughed and slapped each other on the back.

Years later, when I look at that beautiful belt that Jose made for me, I am still amazed that I didn't get an ass-kicking, official reprimand, or something much worse.

Some people may not feel fear. I have heard others say that they only felt it afterward. I was never so lucky. I have felt fear many times, in the midst of the event, totally aware that my next actions would change someone's life (maybe mine) forever.

The laws of our country and of our states provide the authority for your police officers to carry and use deadly force under the circumstances that are outlined in the states' use-of-force laws. All police officers are taught exactly what that fine line is.

They are expected to protect themselves and others from another person's unlawful use of force, and to that degree are authorized to use the force necessary to prevent or stop the aggression, including deadly force, if the other's actions would imminently result in death or serious bodily injury.

Plainly put, if someone is about to wound someone else so seriously that they would be crippled for life or killed, a peace officer has the authority to kill the offender.

A significant factor in this authority is the time element. The act must be <u>imminent</u>, meaning that it is occurring right now or so soon to right now that only immediate action can prevent it.

On a warm summer midnight shift, the call came in from residents who lived near "Hippie Hollow," a clothing-optional county park on Lake Travis. The caller said there was a man throwing rocks at their house and yelling for someone to call the police because his girlfriend had been kidnapped.

In 1977, we sent two-thirds of our on-duty staff. That was me and John Ketchum. John has since gone to work as a game warden for Texas Parks and Wildlife. A really nice and very large man, he was always very calm and spoke with quiet authority.

We arrived at the same time; John quickly interviewed the man and got this story:

The man's girlfriend and he had driven three hours from Houston to spend the day naked in the park. That wasn't unusual; we got lots of business from Houston. They had been befriended by another man at the park and the three of them spent most of the day swimming and relaxing in the sun on the rocky shore. When night drew upon them, they stayed past the curfew and probably smoked pot together. About midnight, the stranger's friendly attitude completely changed. He angrily told the woman that she was going to have sex with him, and when she and her boyfriend objected, the stranger pushed the boyfriend to the ground and patted his back pocket, stating that he had a gun and would use it if the boyfriend got back up. The stranger forced the girl into their car, and they left the park.

When the boyfriend described the car, John and I knew that we had seen it parked partially off the roadway just a half-mile back.

We hauled ass back to where we had seen the car. John was slightly ahead of me, so he pulled into the standard police position behind the vehicle (offset to the left by two to three feet, with wheels turned out) and turned on his spotlight and overhead lights. I took up a position further left, my headlights and spotlight directed on the driver's door.

I stepped out and to the left. John, being aware that he didn't want to walk in front of his headlights and give the suspect a perfect target, exited his driver's door and looped around the back of his car to approach the suspect car on the right side.

John, being the senior officer, had my full confidence in handling this correctly.

He never got the chance.

In a blitz that would have made a defensive football coach proud, a totally nude five-foot woman sprinted out of the passenger side of the car and tackled the six-foot-three-inch, two-hundred-and-thirty-pound John.

For a moment, I was stunned. She took him down by wrapping her arms and legs completely around him while running at full speed. They were in a wiggling pile on the shoulder of the road. The suspect was now my responsibility.

My attention was completely focused on the suspect. Perfectly illuminated by my lighting pattern, I could see him very clearly. My gun was drawn and I ordered him to show me his hands. Instead, his shoulders moved furiously and he asked me "What'd I do, What'd I do?"

"Hands!" I yelled, "Show me your hands!" The stupid son of a bitch continued to manipulate something below the door frame; I could see his arms and shoulders moving desperately to do something. I knew he was fumbling for the gun on the floorboard.

Still, he kept staring at me and asking "What'd I do?"

"Hands!" I yelled the third time. "Show me your hands!"

I was acutely aware that my knowledge of the use of deadly force laws was about to be tested.

I was ready; when he raised the gun above the door frame, I would be justified in using deadly force to prevent his imminent use of deadly force against me.

Until that time, I was not justified.

I would have less than a half second to see and recognize the gun as a gun and not his driver's license or some other innocent object and fire my weapon.

"What'd I do"? he continued.

I knew that my bullet would strike him in his left ear, expanding and fragmenting as it severed the cerebral cortex, ceasing his movement and life.

Slipping into his style of street language, I shouted, "You are gonna do dead, if I don't see your hands right now."

Out, his hands popped through the driver's window, empty and open.

I released the pressure on the trigger.

I was immensely relieved.

"Crawl out the window". He complied. "Face down on the pavement, hands behind your back." He did it.

He was easily cuffed and searched. There wasn't much to search. He was naked from the waist down.

Once handcuffed and secure, I was so relieved that I had not shot this idiot, I could have hugged him.

By this time, John had gotten himself untangled from the woman.

We searched everywhere, but there was no gun. There never was one. It had been a bluff. When he saw the cops pull up behind him, he began trying to pull his pants back on. That's the movement I had thought was reaching for a gun under his seat! And, his attention being on his wardrobe gave the woman the break she needed to make her escape.

I had been very scared as that played out. I knew exactly what could happen and what would happen.

Those few seconds before he obeyed my commands are burnt into my mind.

He was lucky, but I was the one who was really happy.

One afternoon as Sergeant Castro and I were preparing for a 3:00 pm to 11:00 pm shift, off-duty deputy Vann called in. He was at a neighbor's house and needed assistance with a 10-96 subject.

"10-96" means a mental subject. As we raced code three (lights and sirens activated) to Vann's location, Sergeant Castro explained that Vann's next-door neighbor called him at home, said she was having trouble with her seventeen-year-old son and wanted Vann to talk with him. Vann went over, only to be confronted by a high school fullback with a butcher knife. The boy was not allowing Vann into the house to check on the condition of the mother and Vann feared the worst.

It's 1977, so we didn't yet have SWAT yet. LAPD barely had SWAT at this time. We didn't have negotiators. NYPD was just then developing the model that we would eventually use. Even though we were in Austin, Texas, where the need for specialized police teams was first realized: In 1966, Charles Whitman climbed to the top of the University tower and killed sixteen and wounded thirty during a ninety-four-minute killing spree. At that time none of the police departments in the United States had special teams to handle such situations. The Austin Police officers' handguns could not reach the observation deck where Whitman was casually shooting people. Still eleven years later, we still had no special teams.

It was just us.

We arrived and Jose instructed me to wait at the front door, as he was going around back. When he got into position, I was to knock and loudly say "Sheriff's Office." Somehow he knew that the subject would run out the back door when he heard me.

When Jose got into the backyard, he radioed that Vann was back there too and that I should knock and announce.

Boom, Boom, Boom, I hit the door. "Sheriff's Office!"

The garage was next to the front door. It had those tall glass panes that many garage doors have.

In about four seconds, I saw the young man come out the kitchen door into the garage and head for the rear exit door of the garage to egress into the backyard.

When he opened the rear door, Vann and Jose stood with weapons drawn and ordered him to drop the knife.

He held a ten-inch butcher knife in his right hand.

He was tearful and moaning, obviously extremely distraught.

Again, Vann told him to drop the knife.

He stood still and then raised the knife high over his head, tip pointed at them.

He screeched like a wild man, threw the knife to the ground and charged towards the pair of veteran officers in the backyard.

It happened so quickly, that I was absolutely certain one of them would shoot.

Neither did. But neither had time to holster, either. He hit them full force, and they all fell to the ground. Both deputies were struggling with the young man and putting their guns back in their holsters. I sprinted for the backyard.

By the time I got there, they had secured their guns but were losing the fight. This large healthy young man was fixing to whip both of their asses.

It took all three of us to get handcuffs on his wrists and still he fought and kicked us. Vann instructed me to put my handcuffs on his ankles. To my surprise, with just a small pinch of flesh, they fit. We then connected a third set of handcuffs to the pair on his wrists and the pair on his ankles, effectively hogtieing him. We sat on top of him while we breathed.

The mother came out the back door, unhurt. She told us that her son had been displaying unusual angry outbursts over the past weeks and today had broken furniture, beat holes in the wall and threatened her. She didn't know what to do, so she called her deputy sheriff's neighbor.

We transported the boy to the hospital for a mental exam. Years later I would learn he was exhibiting classic symptoms of schizophrenia that mysteriously appeared in young men in the late adolescent years.

Jose lost his favorite tie-tack.

It was understood that even though both deputies would have been justified in shooting and killing the man, neither one had pulled the trigger.

In another jurisdiction, the cops would have shot the young man, the incident would have been on TV and in the newspapers, there would have been a long investigation, and there would have been allegations of police abuse because the police shot and killed an unarmed teenager.

No one except the five of us knew what happened in that backyard that day.

Both of those senior deputies, in less than a second, made the same conscious decision NOT TO SHOOT, a courageous act.

Both men never spoke of it.

I knew they were heroes.

I had joined the Sheriff's Office wanting to do the right thing. I learned that I was not alone. While there was a sizable population of assholes in this agency, occasionally a good guy would get hired. James Riley Book was one of those. He came from Cook County, Illinois, in 1979 and had a thick Chicago accent. His accent and voice tone could piss off some of the locals and old-timers, but James had an honest desire to do the right thing. He also had incredible mental and physical stamina.

He was an ex-Marine and had taught firearms training at Quantico, Virginia. He saw that we had no formal training program at the sheriff's office. Supposedly, every fourth month we would have the next four Fridays for training. The lieutenant or the sergeant was supposed to organize appropriate training for us, it was usually a screw-off job like serving misdemeanor warrants.

James -- we all called him Jamie -- asked if he could set up firearms training. He got approval but with no funding. He worked to find old wooden barricades that we could mount targets on. He befriended a gravel pit owner and got permission for us to shoot on his property and "borrowed" a paper target from the Austin police. Somewhere he found extra ammunition.

On those Fridays, we would shoot. I needed the practice. I was a poor shot. Jamie kept after me to develop good shooting habits and it paid off. Under Jamie's guidance everyone's score improved.

After a few months of shooting, I began to think about other types of training. Another confidence builder, is rappelling.

I talked to Jamie about this and he liked the idea and agreed to help me. I didn't know that he had a significant concern about heights. We got all the ropes and harnesses and webbing, got permission to use the Austin Fire Department's fire tower and taught our ground school with our fellow officers.

Jamie and I then proceeded to the top of the seven-story tower to demonstrate the proper technique. We adjusted his harness, set him on rappel and he stepped backward to the ledge.

Until this moment, I had no idea that heights bothered him at all.

He had his back to the open space below, standing in proper position, facing me.

He said "Tommy." For the first time I could see the concern in his eyes. "Tommy, I don't think I can do this."

I was less than eighteen inches from him, so I said in a low voice, "You are the instructor. There are twenty officers below waiting to learn from your example. Not only can you do this, you are going to do this." We talked for less than thirty seconds about how he knew all the procedures how he had practiced them at low levels and that the mechanics were all the same up here.

I saw him think about it, take a deep breath and step backwards and begin a seventy-foot decent.

His technique was flawless. The rest of the students did fine that day. They had a great instructor.

Chapter Four

Rooftop Risks and Leadership Shifts

Things went along and by 1979 I had been promoted to Sergeant.

The county budget had grown some, as did our staffing. I now had eight to ten deputies assigned to my shift.

As much as I had enjoyed the job of a patrolman, the job of the patrol sergeant was even better.

I had the entire county for my district. I went to wherever the most difficult or exciting call was. I loved driving the rural roads. I knew the shortest and fastest routes from anywhere in our nine-hundred-square-mile jurisdiction. I made it my habit to be the second officer on any call that required a two-deputy response.

I also enjoyed preparing for each day of duty.

I scanned the activity logs of the shifts prior to ours. I would make a report for each day's briefing of where crime had occurred while our group was on duty the day before.

It gave us an idea of what was happening around us. I kept track of the crimes reported both when we were on and when we were off duty. Over a period of months and years, there was an obvious trend. When our shift was on duty, the reported rate of crimes of opportunity went down. Crimes like burglary of homes, businesses and vehicles would drop as much as thirty percent when my guys were on the street. They wanted to do their job, and given some encouragement and some tools, they did.

I also read every crime report to learn the details and reported to our group if there was something of particular concern.

When I read the burglary report of a tire store in Del Valle, it changed the way I thought about burglars. Late at night, these guys had entered the building by cutting a hole through the roof. Once inside, their movement activated the alarm. The responding deputies checked all the doors and windows, found them locked and secure and left the premises, reporting the alarm as "faulty."

The thieves then had all night at their leisure to remove the merchandise.

It wasn't our shift of guys who had been duped, but I was adamant about that not happening to us.

From then on, every time there was an alarm call at a business that had secured doors and windows, I would find a way to get on the roof. I would climb a drain pipe or I would get on top of the fence next to the building and climb to the roof. My thinking was, if I couldn't find a way onto the roof, then neither could the burglars.

I never found any burglars, but at least twice I got more than I had planned on.

The first mishap occurred in the Pilot Knob area. A business alarm was activated, and all doors were locked. I found easy access to the roof, where I was amazed to find a three-foot-by-three-foot hole. I informed the other deputies on the ground of the hole and my intention to enter the building, preparing the deputies for the certain escape attempts of the thieves below.

I went back to the hole and shined my flashlight inside. I saw many plants and some glass walls, no movement or sounds from thieves. Sitting in the hole I braced myself with hands on opposite sides and lowered them until I dropped the remaining four to five feet to the ground.

Certain the thieves would run, I made my presence known by shining my light throughout the interior and stating "Sheriff's Office!"

Nobody ran. Nothing moved.

I looked around a bit more, and now I am able to see the entire office area. I was inside a small glass room in the center of the building. The only other objects in the room with me were plants. I was in an atrium. I looked for the access door and found it, locked from the other side. I inspected the glass walls all the way around, ground to ceiling. Solid, with no openings whatsoever. I looked back up; there was no way I could jump to the roof, and there was nothing inside the atrium for me to stand on. It took a few minutes, but I had to admit the obvious: I was trapped.

I radioed to the troops outside, who naturally informed me that no thieves had made a hasty exit.

"Thanks for the news flash," I thought.

I told them of my predicament, and they informed dispatch that we needed a "key holder" to come to our location. A key holder, as the name implies, is an employee who has the key to the business, normally only called when we have captured criminals in the building or had an access issue of normal concerns.

It was a long and embarrassing wait until I was released. My troops rightfully ribbed me for weeks about it.

A few months later on a cold winter night Bob Mell and I responded to an alarm at a restaurant at 3:00 am, and when I found a ladder leaning against the back roof line, I couldn't resist.

It was a beautiful full-moon winter night in Texas. Just at thirty degrees outside. Nice and crisp.

I climbed the ladder. It was a steep sloped metal roof. The moon made the frost on the metal twinkle.

I stepped off the ladder and began walking up the roof. I took exactly three steps and my feet came out from under me and I landed hard on my right side.

Later, I would come to understand that my leather-soled boots, fresh from inside a heated patrol car, were warm enough to melt the frost on the first and second steps I took. But on my third step, they had a thin layer of ice on the sole. And when you put ice against ice, it's fairly slippery, especially on a slanted metal roof.

I fell and began to slide down the roof. I was on my stomach, a long way from the ladder, sliding towards it, gaining speed. Looking over my shoulder, I was hoping to place both of my feet against the upright portions of the ladder and come to a stop -- I only hooked one side of the ladder with one foot. The ladder began to lean away from the roof, but I came to a stop: One foot dangling in space, the other pushing against the ladder. I tried to get up. That was a bad idea as any movement broke what little friction existed between me and the roof and I would begin to slide again. I had to stay perfectly still.

I could reach my handheld radio, but when I tried to take it out of its pouch, that was too much movement. I began sliding again. I stopped pulling on the radio. Without taking the radio out of the pouch, I mashed the transmit button and said "Bob, come around back."

I didn't explain any further, because it was a county-wide frequency and I didn't want to tell everyone what had happened.

Bob, hearing my voice soft and secretive, thought I must have spotted criminals. He came quietly but carefully and slowly. Finally, I heard him say, from ten feet below, "Sarge? Is that you?" He could see a prone figure dangling partially on and partially off the roof. It looked like his supervisor, but what the hell was going on?

I quickly explained that he needed to steady the ladder or I would slide the rest of the way off.

Once back on solid ground, Bob told me that he was glad that I was all right, but he informed me that he was not going to be able to keep this incident secret. He was going to tell all the other troops and they would tease me unmercifully.

They did. And I finally quit climbing on roofs.

In 1980, Sheriff Raymond Frank lost his reelection bid to Austin Police Department (APD) homicide detective Doyne Bailey.

Frank's second term was tarnished with arguments between him and other county officials. The media had found that he and his female chief deputy of administrative duties had traveled on county money to Houston for a long weekend, supposedly looking for a wanted felon. Only it turns out the felon had long been dead and the warrant was never recalled.

Sheriff Frank also had the habit of making snap decisions that would not have been questioned in the Air Force, but in the liberal environment of Austin, Texas, all decisions were open for review by the press and the public.

He also had some of the old-time staff that no longer needed to be peace officers.

He had brought the Sheriff's Office out of the horse and buggy days, but now it was time for someone to bring it into the twentieth century.

Doyne Bailey was an ordained minister from Arkansas. He had come to Austin and became a police officer. He was known as a police officer with a heart, and he had gained an honest reputation for helping people, regardless of color, income or background.

He created a non-biased Internal Affairs unit that honestly investigated allegations of wrongdoing by staff members. He created a

Public Information position, and insisted that the media know the truth about any situation the Sheriff's Office was involved in.

He brought true experience to our investigations unit and showed them how to manage cases and people.

He created an unbiased hiring procedure and took himself out of the decision process, relying on an in-depth background investigation, fitness testing and oral interview scores to select and rank the most qualified applicants for his agency.

He created our Victim Services unit to help victims (and deputies and their families) find their way through critical incidents and the criminal justice system.

He also had a great passion for training. Doyne was a great instructor himself. He arranged for Jamie Book and some other officers to work full-time on creating lesson plans and obtaining state certification for their courses. Doyne knew that well-trained officers made good decisions.

Officers well trained in defensive tactics would use only the amount of force necessary to affect the arrest.

Officers trained in proper investigative techniques prepared better cases for prosecution.

Officers trained in victimology better understood the victim's perceptions and concerns. Victims who were understood made cooperative witnesses. Cooperative witnesses showed up for trial and testified. Good testimony got convictions. Bad guys went to jail.

The benefits of training were numerous and long-term. Today the men and women of TCSO still enjoy the foundation laid out by Doyne Bailey and Jamie Book.

Doyne also brought in a new chief deputy, Dan Richards -- a man of great integrity, deep solid ethics and insightful management style.

Dan would serve as interim sheriff for six months in 1992, during which time he showed great courage and wisdom. A separate book could be written about this man and his actions.

We entered the 1980s and Austin was growing. We have always enjoyed a beautiful and natural setting on the Colorado River, near hills and creeks, with plenty of parks for camping and hiking. In the eighties the entire nation became aware of the EPA and the Endangered Species Act. As it turns out, Travis County is home to a federally identified species of bird, the golden cheek warbler, which lives almost exclusively in the trees of the western part of the county. They are Ashe Juniper trees that everyone called cedar trees. The trees that my grandfather said were not there in the thirties when he traveled through Central Texas. The trees that any farmer or rancher would cut down because they stole water from other plants that provided shade or grazing for livestock. These are the trees that every non-native was allergic to causing an annual glut in doctors' offices all over Austin every December and January, known as "cedar fever season." The trees that didn't belong there would spread and choke out good trees like the oak and elm.

Now, those trees could not be cut down without following certain federal guidelines to ensure that they were not golden cheek warbler habitat.

None of this was any of my concern until one chilly March day shift began with a call to the new subdivision that was being built west of town, called Steiner Ranch.

The work was being halted by a group of young people who had crept into the construction site under the cover of darkness and had chained themselves to the large pieces of heavy machinery that were being used to push down the trees.

What a scene it was. Twenty young people were padlocked, handcuffed and chained to bulldozers and trucks next to the aluminum frame construction office. About fifteen large and angry equipment operators were yelling at the kids and the kids were yelling back.

It took a few minutes to get the gist of the argument. The youngsters were from Earth First!, a new environmental organization that believed the subdivision creator had bamboozled his authorization from the feds to bulldoze the roads. They believed that the bulldozed roads would threaten the environment of the golden cheek warbler and the construction needed to be stopped.

The construction workers didn't know anything about any damn bird and wanted to get to work, as they were paid by the hour, and they wanted a full forty-hour paycheck for their families.

We had no training in how to handle this.

As I was making my way to the construction office to speak with the construction foreman, one of the bulldozer operators approached me. He showed me a five-gallon can of bearing grease. He said that he thought if we applied enough grease to the kids, we could pull the kids through the chains and then he could go back to work.

I knew that we needed to do something. But that wasn't it.

Luckily for me, the main construction boss on the scene, and his boss in an office downtown, were willing to talk.

They quickly agreed that their employees were "on the clock" and being paid, regardless of the situation.

That announcement made a huge difference in the general tone of the crowd. The employees quit yelling at the kids and began enjoying an extended coffee break on a cool spring morning.

I then walked over to the kids and asked them what they wanted. For the first ten minutes, they told me that they wanted the construction to stop, that they chained themselves to the equipment and had no intention of leaving. Ever.

That didn't make sense, I told them. What are you going to do for food? What are you going to do when it rains? You can't just stay chained to the equipment forever.

That was true, they admitted, and what they really wanted was television coverage.

They had called the local television stations and wanted the film crews to see them chained to the machines so they could get their message out. They wanted the people of Austin to know about the atrocity that was being carried out in this area. What they didn't know was the subdivision owners had purchased and given several thousands of acres to the city for protected parkland in exchange for being allowed to build this subdivision. I didn't know it either.

I checked, and sure enough, two of the three TV stations had film crews on the way to the site.

I explained this to the construction boss and he agreed that his crew could stay on the clock until we had this resolved. I spoke with the big boss in Austin, and he expressed his desire not to file charges for trespassing. He didn't want or need the hassle of criminal proceedings being associated with his work. He just needed us to preserve the peace and return his construction site and equipment to his use.

I then went back out to the kids and explained what we were going to do. I was making this up as I went.

When the film crews got here, I told the kids, we would position the cameras in such a way that they get a good picture of all of them chained to the tractors and equipment. The kids should make statements about the endangered bird and their actions to save it. After a few minutes of filming, I would then direct my officers to approach the youngsters and take them into custody. We would position our patrol cars so that the film crew could get the apprehension, escort and placement inside the marked patrol cars, thereby demonstrating their dedication to this worthy cause.

I asked the kids if that was the kind of coverage they wanted and they agreed it sounded like a plan.

Only one time before the TV crews got there did we have to calm an angry construction worker, but mostly we drank coffee and waited.

After about half an hour, the TV crews got there, got set up and we went to work. The cameras were aimed at the kids in various types of self-inflicted bondage. My deputies and I walked into the frame and began, without any struggle, to unlock the young men and women and place them in handcuffs and lead them to the waiting patrol cars. All caught on film. It was actually boring and the TV crew left even before we finished.

Once we had them all at the patrol cars, I then asked, "Who wants to go to jail and who wants to go home?"

They just blinked for a few seconds.

They hadn't expected that.

Some said they were hungry and cold and just wanted to go home, but about half said they wanted to go to jail.

I told the ones who wanted to go to jail to get in the back seats of the patrol cars and they obeyed. The cars were warm; they liked that. I told the others they could go home, and they quietly went to their cars and left.

My deputies drove off, with their prisoners. I knew that I would call the deputies in about twenty minutes, when they had traveled most of the way to the jail and tell them the owner didn't want to file charges. The deputies would pull over and release the kids downtown, near the University and their homes.

I was just about to congratulate myself when I realized we still had one young man defiantly chained to a bulldozer.

He was an unusual one. He had a U-shaped bicycle lock around his neck and the hydraulic arm of the bulldozer.

He said that he wasn't leaving. I tried to cajole him. He didn't like me. I tried to get him to see the reason. All his friends had gone, and he should, too.

He wouldn't budge.

All right. I told him to quit messing around and give me the key. He had thrown it into the woods he said. He didn't have a key.

He went on to explain that this lock was the toughest on the market, and that it couldn't be cut or sawed apart.

He was staying, he said.

I knew that with the right tools the hydraulic arm could be removed, but that would entail getting a construction worker close to the agitated young man for too long a period of time. It would also take that piece of equipment out of commission for an even longer period of time while the hydraulic arm was being reassembled.

I knew that I could call for our Crime Scene unit to bring a metal detector, but that would take at least an hour to get them on the scene, and then how long would it take to find that damn key?

I needed something quick and effective.

I picked up my handheld radio. "Travis County, contact the Fire Department and tell them I need the Jaws of Life."

The Jaws of Life is a hydraulic tool made for automobile extractions. Basically, huge metal bars that opened and closed like jaws. Used to cut open cars to remove crash victims, it was a lifesaver.

The Fire Department wanted to know what the emergency was. I didn't explain but said that I didn't require a Code Three response, just the Jaws and an operator.

In about ten minutes, the fireman was on the scene in the rescue truck. I pointed to the young man with the bicycle lock around his neck and said, in a loud voice, "We are going to cut that lock off his neck. Let me help you get the equipment set up."

The fireman allowed me to guide him behind the truck, where he said to me in a low voice, "You know, this thing doesn't have that much … ahh…finesse." I told him that it would be okay, to just get the compressor set up and uncoil the hoses.

He did as he was told, and after the compressor was running for about a minute, he picked up the forty-pound Jaws and carried them to the end of the hoses just fifteen feet from the young man.

The young eco-terrorist watched as we attached the Jaws and the fireman pressed the trigger.

"Ka Chong!" The eight-inch-wide sixteen-inch-long jaws slammed open. The sound was so loud and metallic that it echoed off the other pieces of heavy equipment around us.

I nodded my head, and the fireman pressed the trigger again.

"Ka Chong!" They slammed shut.

"Here! Here! I have the key right here!" The kid was screaming to be heard over the roar of the compressor and clanging metal.

"I had it in my shoe. Here!"

I don't remember if he elected to take the ride to jail or whether he went home. But it was over. He unlocked himself, took his bike lock and was gone.

Sometimes we looked for different ways to solve problems. I recall one midnight shift when a drunk was causing problems in a mobile home park. We would get a call, and by the time we responded, he would have disappeared into a trailer, and we couldn't find him. It was very frustrating. Finally, on the third call, we were told that he was at his mom's trailer.

Deputy Don Ledge and I went to her home and asked if her son was there. Yes, he was, but he was sleeping in a bedroom. We explained the problems he had been causing and asked her how we could be assured that he would stay put. She didn't have a clue, but didn't want him in her house.

There was our answer. It was her house, so acting in her interest, we could inform the offender that he was to leave the residence or face being arrested for trespassing. Refusing to leave was grounds for a warrantless arrest.

As we approached the bedroom, Don enhanced the plan by suggesting we take him while he was still asleep.

We tiptoed into the room, whispered, "Jimmy, you have to get up and leave, or we will be forced to arrest you." You guessed it. He failed to comply.

He was on his back. I crawled onto the bed patted his shoulder and said, "Jimmy, you need to roll over." I gave him a nudge and he rolled onto his face. Don took one arm and I the other. We quickly placed the handcuffs on him.

Now he was sort of waking, but still mostly out. We spoke softly and calmly to him, telling him that he was to stand up, everything was okay and that he should walk with us.

Very obligingly, this guy walked himself outside and into the waiting patrol car.

I liked that solution. No fighting, no struggle, and no problem.

So, about four months later on a cold winter midnight shift when we were answering a strange call, I thought the solution might be worth another try.

At a different trailer park at 3:00 am, a male caller said there was a naked woman outside his home. She refused his help and he was concerned. It was below freezing outside.

As we responded to the area, we stopped a man walking out of the subdivision. When questioned, he said that he had been visiting his girlfriend's house when her ex-boyfriend broke in and began beating him. He had run out of the house, he said.

We got him to direct us to the mobile home where this had happened. There in the driveway was her car, windows broken out, tires flattened. Once at the front door, we could see that many of the windows were broken, as well. We knocked and loudly stated "Sheriff's Office!" No one answered the locked front door. After a few minutes we found the totally nude woman hiding in a metal storage shed behind the house.

It was in the low thirties and it was cold. We got her in a blanket and then into a neighbor's house where she told us what had happened.

She had had her new boyfriend over for the evening and they had gone to bed and been asleep when her ex-boyfriend woke them up by hitting them with a wooden club. She fought with the ex for a few minutes before she managed to escape outside. As far as she knew, the ex was still inside her house.

Leaving a deputy with her and her current boyfriend to continue the interview, and receive arriving medical assistance, my buddy Don Ledge and I returned to the trailer.

As the front door was locked, we quietly made our way around the home, looking for an entry. In the back was the air conditioner unit beneath what had to be the window to the master bedroom.

The A/C unit was about three feet tall, and once I stepped up on it I had a clear view into the bedroom. I shone my flashlight and could see a very large man asleep on the bed.

Great, I thought, just like that other time. I motioned for Don to come up to the A/C unit with me. I took out my handcuffs in preparation for another easy arrest. As I turned back to the window to open it, I was surprised by the man. He had opened the window and he was reaching for me!

Out of habit, I placed the handcuffs against his outstretched arm.

The handcuff would not close. They only went partway around his wrist! His wrist was too large. This was a really big guy.

As I was making that realization, he grabbed my hands and backed away. Zip, I was inside with him.

Later, Don would say that he had looked down to be sure of his footing before stepping up with me, and when he looked up again, I was gone.

Don didn't hesitate, he jumped right in. We had a fight on our hands.

This guy was over seven feet tall, weighing close to three hundred pounds, and had come to his girlfriend's house to find her with another lover. Boy, was he pissed!

Apparently, he hadn't been passed out on the bed, he was just taking a little breather.

We tried pressure points, we tried arm locks, and nothing was working. He was whipping our butts. However, he was so large the bed made a block in the middle of the small trailer house bedroom and he would trip over it as Don and I tried to find a weakness in his defenses. As he tripped, walking across the bed and heading for Don, we managed to push him out of the bedroom, into the hallway and leg sweep him to the floor.

He was so big that his shoulders and hips touched both sides of the walls in the hallway. Snugly. Don and I got on his back and forced him face down between the walls. The two of us barely outweighed him, but we got him down and eventually got a pair of flexicuffs on his wrists and feet. We were then able to call for backup and carry the guy out to his ride to jail.

As we left the home, we saw that the house was a total wreck; this guy had broken in and destroyed the furniture, apparently using a kitchen table leg as his weapon to beat the sleeping couple in the bedroom.

Some clever plans are meant to work only once, I figured.

As the patrol sergeant, I was in charge of all field activities.

I loved the work, and I respected and admired the deputies and staff of the Sheriff's Office. It was a great place to work.

So, I couldn't believe it when I came to work one Monday morning on the day shift to find that a landowner had trespassers on his property all day Saturday and Sunday and the weekend shift had told him we couldn't help him!

I asked dispatch for the details and found out that Earth First! was back at work in northwest Travis County.

This time, they had decided that there was a certain cricket that should be on the endangered species list but wasn't, and that this cricket lived in some shallow limestone caves on some property that was being developed as a subdivision.

They had effectively stopped the use of any heavy equipment on the property by informing the property owner that they had members living in the caves and that the weight of a bulldozer or other large machine could collapse the caves and kill the Earth First! Member.

Not wanting any negative publicity, much less a wrongful death suit, work had come to a standstill.

The day shift had been working our days off and had been notified of the situation. I was told that their sergeant had been briefed on the situation and that he had concluded that there was nothing the Sheriff's Office could do to remove the protestors from the caves. They had left the property owner with trespassers on his property.

State law requires that peace officers take action. In part it states "It is the duty of every peace officer to preserve the peace within the officer's jurisdiction. To effect this purpose, the officer shall use all lawful means. The officer shall: prevent or suppress crime; and arrest offenders without warrant in every case where the officer is authorized by law, in order that they may be taken before the proper magistrate or court and be tried."

I was certain that we could and should do something.

While civil disobedience is a nonviolent crime, and in some cases it is a valuable and necessary act to bring public awareness to significant wrongness, this situation just seemed like unnecessary harassment by Earth First! and unresponsiveness by the previous shift. It made me adamant that we would do something.

If the cricket should be on the endangered species list, do the work to get it included. If it shouldn't, go find some other mission to be passionate about.

In the eighties the Japanese were killing whales by the thousands. The rainforest of Brazil was being burnt every day. Human slaves were being worked in factories in China. There were plenty of issues to protest other than crickets.

Central Texas is honeycombed with limestone caves. Under a few inches of topsoil, the underground is more like a sponge made of soft rock than "regular" large caves. The holes in these local caves were as small as a few millimeters to a few feet.

A cave large enough to actually stand up in was unusual. As a kid, I explored a few that were close to home. The explorer had to slither on his or her belly across sharp stones and muddy floors to navigate small tight passageways. Nothing like Carlsbad or Longhorn or the recently discovered Natural Bridge Caverns. No big wondrous rooms, just dirty muddy nooks and tubes to pull yourself through.

Small caves were neither unusual nor much fun in Travis County.

We drove to the property and were greeted by the property owners and Earth First! members.

The property owner was frustrated and angry, which was exactly what the kids wanted. I assured him that the Sheriff's Office would take action and that we wouldn't stand by while a crime was being committed in our presence.

I asked the kids which caves held their co-conspirators. While they could have refused to tell me the location of the caves and it would have taken days to locate all of them on this two-thousand-acre subdivision, they instead took us directly to the cave entrance.

There was only one cave and one girl inside the cave. After asking some logistical questions -- like how much food was inside, how human waste was handled and how long they had been inside -- I decided that I would go in the cave and get her out.

It was just this one college girl. Skinny and dirty and probably hungry.

The food was delivered by her friends whenever they remembered to make the twenty-five-mile drive from Austin. They had incorrectly determined that her waste could be placed in one corner of the cave, in the ground. Her presence had had more of an adverse effect on the environment than any overhead construction ever could have.

I took off my gun belt, badge and name tag, anything that could get snagged while crawling through tight spots.

As I entered, I could hear scuffling sounds from the girl. She was trying to crawl to a secluded spot to hide from me.

The cave had a very low ceiling of about two and a half feet but was spread out and had about as much square footage as a two-bedroom house.

She could not go far.

I wiggled down to her spot and introduced myself. She introduced herself and said that she wasn't leaving without a huge fight and that in the confines of the cave both of us would be battered and bruised.

I believed her and told her that I had no intention of dragging her out. I didn't want a fight. I was here to talk.

And that's what we did for maybe thirty or forty-five minutes. We talked about the crickets, the weather, local politics and the world in general.

After a while, I asked her if she was ready to go and she said that she was.

We gathered up her few personal belongings -- a dim flashlight, a bedroll, a one-gallon jug of water and a roll of toilet paper -- and climbed out into the sun.

We were greeted by other cops, her friends and the landowner.

Her friends were aghast. "Where is the evidence of police brutality?" they demanded. "Where are your injuries?"

Their hidden agenda for providing me with her exact location was this: they expected a bloody and beaten little girl to be dragged from the cave, crying and mistreated by a jackbooted Nazi, so she could be paraded in front of cameras as evidence of the tyranny of the establishment.

She sheepishly told them that she had wanted to come out. When that didn't satisfy her friends, she told them that she feared that my aftershave was damaging to the crickets and that she had to come out with me to save the bugs.

"Whatever." I thought to myself.

The peace was preserved and there were no injuries.

Chapter Five

The Rising Waters

Memorial Day 1981. Austin now had about three hundred thousand folks calling it home, and maybe another one hundred thousand in the unincorporated areas that we patrolled.

I was working the 3:00 pm till 11:00 pm shift and my Lieutenant Hap Marvel had decided to spend the evening on the street.

This meant that I had to do his job and sit in the office as the Watch Commander.

It was supposed to be training to be a lieutenant.

Every police agency has such a position; this is the guy or gal who is technically in charge of the entire law-enforcement operation during that tour of duty. He or she is the place where the buck stops.

Mostly they field calls from pissed-off citizens who couldn't understand why we were not going to send a deputy to their non-criminal problem, such as their neighbor's cat using their front yard as its litter box, or whiny media types who wanted to know the deceased person's name so they could report it before the family had been located and politely notified.

In our position we also took and recorded bonds for the jail, acted as the notary public for sworn statements from officers, helped with the overflow of incoming emergency calls and provided relief for the solitary dispatcher on the radio when they had to use the restroom.

Not a very fun duty.

It was raining and had been raining for a few days. It always rains here in the spring.

About 9:00 pm Hap radios from the gas pumps at Tenth and Lamar, a few blocks from the downtown courthouse headquarters.

He tells me and the other deputies that the low-lying area of Shoal Creek near the county gas station is starting to flood and recommends that the deputies get fuel at locations other than this convenient downtown spot.

No problem here, he says, while parked at the pumps, the water is only at his patrol car's wheels. He radios that he will wait there until the water goes down, then drive across the street and up the hill to the courthouse.

I radioed to him and reminded him that he could drive out the other direction and immediately be going up a steep hill on Tenth Street towards Baylor Street that would take him twenty feet above his current location.

He radios back that he will just wait it out.

I started to explain to him the directions to drive out of that residential neighborhood and across the Fifteenth Street bridge to get to the courthouse, but before I could, I noticed that all the incoming telephone lines were lit, and our single call taker was pantomiming for help.

I began answering the phone.

Panicked people from all over the county are calling about rising water.

Folks in eastern Travis County on Walnut Creek were calling to say that the water was coming inside their homes and they worried that it would rise high enough to get inside the electrical outlets. They want to know what they should do.

A man on Lake Austin calls to say that the lake has risen so much that his ski boat has floated up to the back of his house and is bumping up against the wall; he wants to know if the river authority has been notified and wonders if they will be opening additional flood gates.

A man and a woman on the west side of Travis County call to say that the creek behind their house has risen and is washing the bricks off the exterior of the house.

These calls were worrisome, and we offered assistance and sent responders to those calls, but the hard calls were the dozens of stranded motorists caught in the low-water crossings all over the city and county.

Hardly anyone had a cell phone then, so we dispatched our patrol officers to check each low-water crossing in their district. Upon their arrival, many found motorists stuck in the creek, in danger of being washed downstream. Our troops had no training in swift-water rescue and had no equipment; they had only their desire to help people and their own ingenuity to make the rescues they made that night. They all worked hard that night.

In the headquarters, we were busy, sending patrol cars to the motorists and coordinating with the fire departments.

Then I remembered Hap.

"Unit 10" I called him using his radio identifier.

It had been long enough that if he had driven out the other side he would have been here at the courthouse by now.

"Unit 10, go ahead." He responded. It was just another day.

"Where are you? Have you driven out?" I asked. No, he hadn't. I asked how high the water was and he began by telling me that he had taken his wallet out of his back pocket and placed it, along with his briefcase and other essentials from inside the car on top of the trunk.

How deep is the water? I asked. It was just above knee deep, he said. It was inside the patrol car still parked at the pumps. But not to worry, he said. The water would soon recede and he would drive out then. "Hap, Walkout, up the hill." I had dropped all pretense of using official radio protocol. I was worried about him. "I will send a patrol car to get you."

"No, don't waste a car for me, I'll be okay," He said.

I went back to answering the phones.

It was another long thirty minutes before I was able to get away from the phones long enough to call Hap again.

This time, he said that the patrol car was probably going to float away.

Damn! How high is the water?

About at his waist, he responded.

"Hap! There is a county bus with an exterior luggage ladder parked there at the pumps. Climb the ladder and get on the roof of the gas station, now! Hap?...Hap, did you copy it?...Hap?"

The phones were still ringing nonstop, but in a few minutes the oncoming shift of officers, call-takers and dispatchers would be arriving.

As soon as another supervisor arrived, I told them I was leaving to go look for Hap. I took Deputy Will Bilson with me. A nice country deputy, very faithful and hardworking.

First, we drove directly west from the courthouse, down Tenth Street and we were stopped by a raging torrent that used to be a small damp place that had a bridge over it. In fact all of Lamar Boulevard was whitewater crashing and roaring loudly toward Town Lake a mile further downstream. I could just make out the top of the handrails along the sidewalk of the Tenth Street bridge. The water had to be almost three feet over the roadway; the bridge was normally ten feet above the creek bed below. There was a lot of water moving in front of us.

We turned around and approached from Fifteenth Street. Fifteenth Street crosses the creek and the large parallel roadway, Lamar Boulevard, from a bridge with thirteen feet of clearance under it. We stopped the car on the bridge and got out to look downstream toward Tenth Street and Hap's last known location. The rain was falling too heavily to see that far, but I could see the creek was out of its banks and flowing right through the middle of the House Park football stadium below.

We continued across the bridge and turned back to the east to come downhill on Twelfth Street and turned then on Baylor to get behind the gas station from the uphill side.

We got out of the truck about one hundred feet from the gas station and I hollered "Hap!" "Hap!"

I heard a response that I couldn't make out. I hollered again. Again we heard someone respond. But the response was uphill from behind us.

"Hap? Hap, is that you?"

"Yeah its me," an unfamiliar voice answered. "I need help."

The realization came to me that we were in an area loaded with homeless folks, and the rising water would have displaced them from their usual under-bridge dry spots. Yes, the guy was probably wet, cold and needed help, but he was uphill from us and, therefore not in immediate danger of drowning.

"You aren't Hap. Shut up!"

He wouldn't shut up though, every time I yelled for Hap, this asshole would respond, as if we were playing a game of Marco Polo.

"Hap!"

"Over here."

"Not you, Hap!'

"Here I am."

Damn.

I quit yelling and began formulating what little I could for a rescue plan.

We could see the silhouette of the gas station, but it was raining so hard that even with our spotlights and flashlights, we couldn't make out if Hap was on the roof.

I had brought some nylon rope with us.

Behind the gas station was a fenced lot. The chain-link fence around the lot was ten feet tall with three strands of barbed wire above that. The fence was leaning over in the rush of the water; the top strands were still above water.

I took off my gun belt and boots and put them in the car. I tied the rope around my waist and gave the other end to Deputy Bilson. I told him to hang on to me. I was going to crawl down the fence to the gas station and see if Hap was there.

I walked into the water. It was surprisingly cold. I grabbed

the fence and began pulling myself along it. I held the top wire in my hands and stuck my toes in the chain-link sections below.

After what seemed like a long time, I neared the side of the gas station. The water pressure against my chest was incredible. I held tightly to the fence.

I looked back to see how Deputy Bilson was doing.

To my surprise, he was right beside me, also clinging to the fence!

"What the hell are you doing here? You are supposed to be holding the other end of the rope."

The rope had not been long enough, he said. When I got to its end, He held on tightly. He yelled that I was out of rope; I hadn't heard him over the roar of the water and droning rain. Apparently, the pressure of the water had untied my knot and when my end of the rope went slack, he pulled the rope back in, put it in the car and followed me out onto the fence.

"Alright, let's try to get to the building." Another ten to fifteen feet down the fence and we would be next to the gas station. It might be possible to gain the roof from the fence.

We yelled for Hap and got no response.

I had some experience with flood water.

My best friend, Rod Patterson grew up on one hundred acres in western Travis County that had a crooked stretch of Barton Creek running through it. Below seventy-foot bluffs, winding through limestone canyons, was whitewater after every good rain.

We played in that creek all the time. First as seven-year-olds we tentatively explored its wonders, careful not to let his parents know where we had spent our afternoon. They had warned us many times to stay away from such a dangerous place. As the years passed, we enjoyed the seasonal floods of spring, fall and winter that would bring deep, fast water to us. Even recently, Rod and I had great times on this beautiful creek.

We had learned the difference between fast water and flood water. Fast water would smash you into the rocks and drag you along the bottom and when it dropped off of waterfalls it could create an underwater eddy that would suck you down and hold you under. Fast whitewater could be read. A "V" pointing at you as you approached indicated an obstruction just under the surface. A "V" pointing away from you would indicate a trough.

Flood water would do this too, but with added extras.

Besides being brown instead of white, flood water had underwater hazards like submerged trees, roots, bushes or barb wire fences that would tangle you and hold you underwater.

You would never see the underwater object until it had you, and then you would have to be able to untangle yourself from its grip while holding your breath, or obviously drown.

We had swum in flood waters many times over the years. We had built rafts from trees and rope, we had skipped school on rainy days and drug our canoe down to the creek for day-long wet and cold adventures.

Like so many of our experiences, Rod and I were strong enough and lucky enough to come home after being close to real danger.

Clinging to the fence with Will, I thought about another hazard of flood water that was snakes and ants. Fast-rising water washes snakes, fire ants and other critters from their dens or mounds looking for something dry to climb up on. That something would be us. I eyed the deep, fast water that was up to our necks, with only our toes and fingers holding us from being washed away. Was that a snake? Or just another broken tree branch?

As I was assessing our situation, I saw something I had never seen before in flood water.

The soda water machine. It had been located on the side of the building. It popped up from being totally under the water. Just now freed from its lag bolts in the concrete. It was less than six feet away. Its bright backlit display advertising refreshment was blinding in the dark rainy night. I stared at it in wonder and disbelief. It bobbed next to us for just a few seconds, and then leaned over in the push of the water, stayed still for about one second, then the lights went out and it floated off, having its electrical cord finally pulled from the outlet.

An underwater danger that I hadn't dealt with in the country setting of Barton Creek. Electricity. In this urban environment, there was a danger that wouldn't give us a few seconds to untangle.

I looked across the back lot, the flooded streets and the river of what had been the driveway to the gas station. I wondered what power lines had been brought down by rushing water, uprooted trees and the heavy rains.

I yelled for Hap and got no answer; I looked at Will and said that we had to go back. It was time to get out of the water.

Underwater trees and a few snakes were one thing. Underwater voltage was something entirely different.

We climbed back across the fence to the safety of our car. We drove back to Twelfth Street and there was an off-duty Parks and Wildlife game warden with his fishing boat on a trailer behind his pickup.

He was attempting to launch the boat into the torrent.

It was dark, it was raining hard and the water was moving very fast.

Under calm conditions, in daylight it is not easy to launch a boat by yourself.

We spoke for a few minutes, me telling about Hap and his last known location and explaining that the best plan was for him to get in the boat while it was still on the trailer.

I would back the boat only far enough into the water to submerge the propeller, he would then start the engine and wave at me when he was sure the engine was warm and wouldn't stall. I would then back a few more feet into the water and slam on the brakes, the boat would slide the rest of the way off the trailer and he would be launched.

He agreed.

When he waved, I wondered if the engine was warm enough. Losing power in this current would put him at risk of being washed under a low bridge, or crashed into a building or getting tangled in who knows what.

I stomped on the brake and he and the boat slid off into the rainy night.

I pulled the now-drifting boat trailer partially out of the water.

Will and I were soaked and now we are beginning to feel the wind blowing through our polyester uniforms.

We waited just a few minutes, and the P&W officer reappeared; motoring against the current back to us, he had Hap and two other guys!

He pulled close to us and threw a rope that Will caught; we pulled and held the boat steady against the flood, and the three jumped from the boat.

The others were a homeless guy and an employee of the nearby health food store.

"Where were you?" I asked Hap. He had climbed the luggage ladder and got on top of the roof, but he had dropped his handheld radio in the water and it had quit working right after our last conversation. He had heard us yelling, but apparently, we could not hear him respond. He added that the patrol car, his gun, briefcase and everything was gone, lost downstream.

Two days later the marked patrol car was pulled from Town Lake.

But for now, the five of us were cold and shivering. We were becoming hypothermic.

We had to get out of the weather and the wet clothes. The P&W guy told us he would be all right and he pushed away and into the rush of water to look for other rescues.

I never saw him again. I never learned his name. I knew that he had rescued many people that night. Once it was over we learned that thirteen people died in flood-related incidents all over the county. It would have been many more if not for him.

While working midnight shifts, when I was going to get out of my car, I always parked in the dark area of the restaurant or convenience store. A good friend and deputy sheriff who had served in the Marines in Vietnam, Charles Larson, had told me that we were just giving away our location to any bad guys who would drive by, if we parked in front where the lights shone on our cars.

By parking in the dark, we maintained a certain amount of unknown presence with burglars and thieves who worked the midnight shifts. If they didn't know exactly where we were, they had to be extra careful and may even leave our area to steal something somewhere else.

If we needed a private conversation with another staff member, we went to the nearest pay phone. Nobody had a cell phone.

We had the numbers of various pay phones memorized and would tell the radio dispatcher our location by stating the last four numbers of the telephone number at that spot. The dispatcher would then call that number.

Ninety-nine-Eleven was actually 836-9911, the Seven-Eleven store at Braker Lane and Interstate 35. Ninety-eight seventy-eight was actually 892-9878, the U-Tot-Em on US 290 in Oak Hill. In all, we probably had twenty or thirty phone numbers memorized. It served two purposes. One, back then no agency had encrypted radio transmissions; all the bad guys had radio scanners and listened to every word we said. By using a code number instead of saying on the radio, "I will be out of my car at this gas station." we maintained a small bit of edge on the bad guys. And it saved us the cost of the pay phone for Radio to call us. When I started with TCSO, it was a dime. We didn't get paid much and that was money.

One midnight shift, I was in Del Valle and needed to talk with my lieutenant on the phone. I drove to the nearest convenience store. I had approached the store from a residential area, sort of from the rear. I parked on the dark side of the store, instead of in the light in the front. I checked the parking lot, saw that it was empty and radioed my location for the lieutenant to call me.

The pay phones were outside, at the corner of the building on my side.

I walked over and answered the ringing phone.

We had been talking for a few minutes when a private security guard pulled up in his marked car. He parked directly outside the front door (the shortest distance to walk, you know) got out of his car, waved at me and entered the store.

I waved back and continued my conversation.

My concentration was soon broken by the sound of the door opening and a high-pitched screaming, "Robbery! Robbery!" The screams had a peculiar lilt to the tone. Unusual for a Texas community, it sounded Indian or Pakistani. It was.

I looked at the doors and saw three people running straight at me.

In the front was a young man wearing a white T-shirt with the word "Dangerous" on it in red letters. Next in line was a man wearing a store smock and waving a revolver over his head. Last in this running lineup was the uniformed security guard.

They were less than twenty feet away when I first heard "Robbery!" running directly at me they had closed that distance quickly.

I unholstered my gun and said the magic words that made the young man in front come to a halt. He knew that any wrong move on his part and I would pull the trigger of the .357 magnum pointed at his head.

He stopped and I told him to turn around and place his hands behind his back. He complied and I handcuffed him.

The store clerk continued to yell/scream the single word "Robbery" over and over.

I took the gun from the clerk and told him that everything was all right and to try to calm down.

I searched the suspect and then took him to my car seat-belted him into the front seat and locked the doors.

I went back to the phone and picked up the swinging receiver.

I was pumped full of adrenaline. An armed robbery had just fallen on top of me!

I was lucky enough to capture the bad guy without firing a shot, and no one was injured!

Lucky with a capital "L," as it turns out.

I had failed to perform the standard review of the illuminated interior of the store when I had approached from the rear.

When I saw no cars in the lot, I <u>assumed</u> no customers were inside! A huge mistake!

Another thing that Charles Larson had taught me was that I should drive by convenience stores and look directly inside and see if the clerk was calmly standing behind the counter without ever driving into the lighted parking lot.

By doing this, you could periodically check the status of your late-night clerks. If you didn't see them standing behind the counter, it was time to stop, go in and check on them.

I had not done that with this store. I had made the almost fatal assumption that it was okay, because no cars in the parking lot meant no robbers in the store. A very bad decision on my part!

As I interviewed the clerk and security guard, I learned that the robber had walked into the store when no one else was inside.

He had spent a long ten minutes threatening the clerk and demanding money, cigarettes and sunglasses. He was extremely nervous and told the clerk several times that he would shoot him if he pushed the panic button to summon the police.

Banks have panic buttons, not a little mom-and-pop all-nighter. This indicated the robber's experience level was low, meaning that he was uncertain of the situation and circumstances, which meant that he would be very volatile and reactive. A dangerous combination.

During the robbery, before my arrival, a customer drove into the parking lot.

The robber told the clerk not to say anything or he would kill him and placed his gun under his T-shirt.

Both the robber and the clerk greeted the customer, who made his purchase and left.

The robber once again drew his gun and accosted the clerk. He again told him not to push the panic button or he would shoot him.

The robber ordered the clerk to gather several items from behind the counter for him. This is when I was parking on the side of the building.

Then the security guard drove up and parked in front.

Both the robber and the clerk could see it was a marked private security officer.

The robber told the clerk he was lucky that it was not the Sheriff's Office. If it had been, he would have to kill the clerk and the deputy!

The robber placed the gun under his T-shirt, in the small of his back. He turned his back to the clerk and greeted the security guard as he entered the store.

"Good evening, officer. "

The clerk saw his opportunity; he stretched across the counter and grabbed the gun from the robber's pants.

Triumphantly, he held the gun high for the security guard to see and announced, "He is robbing me!"

The security guard responded, "This store isn't on my rounds. You will have to talk to the deputy outside on the phone."

The robber decided it was time to run. And the clerk decided it was time to pursue. The security guard came along to see what was next.

Why the robber exited the front doors and took a hard left turn, I still do not understand.

I would later learn that he lived in a run-down mobile home off to the right. Why not run that way?

Or having no car, why not run for the highway and hope to hitchhike from the scene by heading straight out the doors?

But he turned to the left, which put him on a collision course with me.

What a series of circumstances and luck!

It was lucky the robber didn't shoot the clerk when the security guard drove up and then got in a shootout with the security guard and/or me.

It was luck that the clerk was able to gain control of the gun and not fumble it, causing the robber to begin shooting.

It was luck that when the robber turned left, he wasn't armed and the confrontation came to a sudden halt when I confronted him, instead of a shootout.

It was lucky the robber didn't finish the robbery early, walk out, see me with my head down talking on the phone, and just shoot me without me ever seeing him.

There are so many other ways this could have played out. The clerk, the security guard and I were all very lucky that night -- lucky with a capital "L" that had gold wings and a bright light shining on it!

I always tried to be a good cop. The kind of cop that I wished had stopped me in traffic when I was a kid. The kind of cop who helped people. The kind of cop who solves problems. The kind of cop who would look for a way not to arrest someone, but to get the situation resolved instead.

Even though I tried to be a good cop, I ended up being investigated by Internal Affairs.

We got a call about a disturbance in the parking lot of an apartment complex.

I and Deputy Randy Wilson and I arrived to find a mechanic and an Asian man arguing about the payment required for some car repair the mechanic had performed.

I usually liked these sorts of problems. They were communication problems, really. And with a little bit of listening skills and a good knowledge of Texas law, I could explain what the misunderstanding was and how we were going to solve the problem.

After listening to both parties, we figured out that the mechanic was holding a mechanic's lien on the man's car, as the man had refused to pay what he thought was too much for the repairs.

Thus the mechanic was refusing (rightfully) to release the car until the guy paid for the repairs.

I explained this to the car owner, saying that he had made an agreement and the law gave the mechanic the authority to hold the car until the car owner upheld his part of the agreement.

He finally saw the light and said that he would go to his apartment to get his check book. He needed his keys to unlock his apartment door.

I turned to the mechanic and asked him to hand over all but the car keys.

He refused!

The mechanic, who had a droopy mustache that was intended to obscure his awful yellow protruding teeth, told me that the law said he didn't have to release anything to that guy.

I said, "No, that's not how it works. You have the right to hold the car until this man pays you or makes reasonable arrangements to pay. You do not have the right to hold any other property, including the house keys."

He looked right at me, spoke through that poor excuse for a mustache and said "No, the law says I do not have to give him anything."

He also spoke with an accent that I was unfamiliar with.

I asked him where he was from and he told me that he had recently moved here from Kentucky.

Well, maybe the laws were different in Kentucky, I explained, but here in Texas, I could assure him how the law worked.

Nope, with his flapping mustache, he said, he wasn't giving the guy anything out of the car.

I saw this as just another level of misunderstanding. I was going to successfully get the mechanic to see the reason. This sort of problem-solving was challenging, yet rewarding.

It's simple, really. Let the guy have the house keys and he would get his money. Intentionally keeping the guy's house keys was a criminal act, theft.

I politely began explaining that the laws were different here in Texas and he was going to have to give the guy his keys.

Through his misshapen and wiggly mustache and stained and crooked teeth, he said no, he didn't have to and he wasn't going to.

I started to speak again, but this time he interrupted me to tell me that he knew the law and that he didn't have to give the guy "jack squat."

Looking back, I guess it was about there that it started going downhill.

Here was this ugly uneducated backwoods hillbilly from Kentucky telling me what the Texas law said. I was a good Texas cop and by now had eleven years on the street.

I tried to keep my cool, but it must have gotten away from me.

I gave him the ultimatum.

"Give the man his keys or go to jail."

He began telling me that the law gave him the right to keep everything inside the car.

I interrupted him, said a few words to him to explain that the conversation was over, spun him around and put my handcuffs on him.

Randy booked him while I impounded his truck.

He went to jail, his truck was impounded and I gave the car owner his house keys.

About two weeks later I got a call from Internal Affairs officer William Sassom.

The IA officer had been carefully selected by Doyne Bailey because of the high degree of ethics and reputation for fair treatment of the deputies he investigated.

I had known William since his first employment with the Sheriff's Office. He had been a dispatcher on my shift and I saw him promoted to deputy where his first assignment was working for me at Willie Nelson's 1979 Fourth of July picnic directing traffic.

He and I respected each other and I had no intentions of being anything but truthful.

I knew that I had been rude and maybe even disrespectful and I wasn't going to lie about it.

As I was saying this to William, he stopped me.

"Tommy, I am not asking you to make a statement or to say anything that may implicate you. Allow me to read you what this man accuses you of first."

Okay, that sounds fair.

"Now, this first part doesn't sound so bad." William continued. He read, "Then he called me a back woods hillbilly from Kentucky and said that I didn't know anything about Texas law. "

William looked at me over the top of the statement, "That's not real bad, certainly a little rude, but it's this next part that, if you said this, then it is probably going to result in disciplinary action."

"I'll be honest, William. What does he say I said?"

"He says that you called him a vulgar name. He says that you called him a snaggletooth son of a bitch."

I smiled and shook my head; William smiled too, in relief that his old sergeant wasn't going to get in trouble, after all.

I could see the surprise on his face, as I said, "No, William, he is mistaken. I didn't call him a snaggletooth son of a bitch, I called him a buck tooth mother fucker!"

I accepted the recommended disciplinary action without any complaints.

Chapter Six

Grit, Brotherhood, and Tragedy

There are some stories of the Sheriff's Office that I was not present for but happened to friends of mine and need to be told.

A defining episode of early Sheriff's Office business is about Deputy Ricky Morris and his encounter at the Blue Front Bar in Manor, Texas.

Ricky, the nephew of a local musical celebrity, had asked Sheriff Frank for a job and was placed on patrol.

As a young man patrolling the roads of the county in the early seventies Ricky had taken to heart the advice his older more experienced officers had offered him about the Blue Front Bar.

This bar was located in Manor, Texas, a city fifteen miles east of Austin. It was a historic black community that was founded in the early eighteen hundreds. My father, who had served as county attorney for Travis County, had told me that fully one-third of all the cases he prosecuted during the nineteen-sixties came out of incidents that occurred at the Blue Front Bar. Assaults, knifings, shootings, robberies and all sorts of disturbances were common.

It was a rough nightclub and had a serious reputation.

Upon hearing this story from another officer, the story was so incredible that I went to Ricky and asked him how it happened. This is how he told it:

Late one Saturday night, when patrolling the east side of the county, with backup at least forty-five minutes away, young Ricky got a call of a disturbance at the Blue Front and he recalled the words the older guys had told him:

"If you have a call at the Blue Front bar, take your shotgun with you."

Like all the other officers, Ricky had no training in the use of the shotgun. No familiarization with the range, no prior use, nothing.

As a Texas peace officer, it was assumed that the officer had firearms experience and such a simple thing as a sawed-off twelve gauge pump shotgun, loaded with double-aught buckshot, didn't need instructions.

That was how it was back then. Many assumptions, few officers, less training.

Ricky got out of his car and took his shotgun from its stand and racked a round into the chamber. He said the music was deafening outside in the parking lot.

He walked across the gravel driveway to the front door and made up his mind that he was going inside.

He told me that as he stepped inside the front door, he realized that he didn't know if the safety was on or off on the shotgun. With the gun held at port arms, barrel pointed up, his attention on the jammed dance floor of writhing bodies and thundering music, he squeezed the trigger.

He said the effect was instantaneous.

The shotgun went off, blowing a huge hole in the ceiling.

The sound was even louder than the music being played.

The explosion thundered in the ears of everyone in the bar. His ears were ringing.

Little bits of plaster rained down on him, smoke from the barrel swirled as he stood absolutely still looking at all the potential suspects.

The music was turned off.

One hundred black people in the bar were looking at a slightly built white man wearing the required cowboy hat and holding a shotgun. No one was moving.

Ricky said, "Their eyes were like saucers."

I asked him: What did he do? What did he say?

He said it was very quiet and everyone was just staring at him, and he had to say something to explain, so he said, "I am new and I am scared and don't nobody move."

Whatever had happened about the disturbance was over: no one at the bar had any complaints and no one knew who called the cops.

Everyone was very polite and very cooperative. Ricky said they didn't even ask him to pay for the damage to the ceiling.

He said that it actually worked out okay.

He did admit that it was one of the incidents that had him request a desk job working in the fiscal section of the sheriff's office.

Sad things happen too.

Charles Larson came to work for the Sheriff's office in the fall of 1977. He had served two tours of duty in Vietnam, then came home to Austin and worked for seven years with the Austin Police Department. He quit APD due to some beef with superior officers and came to work for us. It was a bountiful gift for us.

Chuck's seven years of street experience and four years of combat experience gave him depth and maturity beyond anything I had seen at the Sheriff's office. He was the first person that had talked about such things as "tactics" or "officer safety issues."

I recognized right away that I could learn a lot from this guy and offered him guidance and insight on dealing with the politics and brass of the Sheriff's Office. He accepted my advice as I accepted his.

We became fast friends. On or off duty, he had something to tell me or show me. Like how not to drive up to a convenience store on the midnight shift, or why it was better to leave your parking lights on when leaving your patrol car at night.

He opened my eyes about such everyday occurrences as where to stand when knocking on the door of an apartment to better ways to extract an unwilling person from behind the wheel of a car.

His informal training and insight have certainly kept me safe and may even have saved my life many times over.

For a laugh one Christmas season, Chuck and I took my mother and a friend of hers to an adult shop to look for novelties or gag gifts.

While I was having a lot of fun watching Mom ask the clerk, "What is that?" I noticed that Chuck had tucked himself deep into a corner of the tiny shop. He seemed real interested in something, but I couldn't tell what.

Mom and her friend, Ollene, picked out a few stocking stuffers and as we left the store Chuck caught up to us on the sidewalk outside.

"What happened to you?" I asked.

Chuck had recognized a plainclothes APD detective in the store with us and didn't want to be seen by him. Chuck thought that his ex-coworker wouldn't believe that he was escorting my sixty-year-old mother and her friend, and would instead think Chuck was a pervert.

We laughed almost all the way home.

Years passed and I was promoted to sergeant and moved to another shift.

I was off duty, at home, when I got the call.

Chuck had been shot while on a traffic stop. Another deputy had found him outside his car, bleeding from a gunshot wound to his neck.

He was alive and they transported him to the hospital. Little else was known.

Every cop in Central Texas was on the hunt.

Our small headquarters on the first floor of the courthouse was packed with representatives from other agencies and off-duty deputies like me, APD guys who had worked with Chuck, state troopers and dozens of others.

We all wanted to help.

A guard of officers was posted in the hospital room. We didn't know if the suspect had a grudge for Chuck and might try to finish the job.

I was one of the officers who was tasked with locating and reviewing every report and traffic ticket that Chuck had ever written, to compile a list of suspects that may have had previous dealings with him.

We had no computers back then; all reports were on paper and filed chronologically. No reference to the reporting officer.

Using the old duty rosters, we knew what dates and times he had been working for those past three years and began pulling and reviewing every one of those reports.

There was a lot of activity that night, but the break came about at dawn when a woman had escaped her rapist kidnapper in a city about one hundred miles from Austin.

The victim had remained calm during her ordeal, so as time passed, her captor had come to trust her. When they stopped for gas at a small country store, she asked to use the restroom and he had allowed her out of the car. She ran for help.

She told her story, and the bad guy, Ricky Ellison, was captured without a fight.

She had been the second rape victim of this crazy young man that night. The first was still being investigated by the Austin Police, when the second victim was taken captive in her own car by Ricky and driven out of town. Ricky had just stopped the car on the shoulder of US 183 to rape the victim when Chuck, traveling in the other direction had spotted them.

Even though it was close to the end of his tour of duty, Chuck turned around to help what had all the appearances of being a stranded motorist.

She told us that when Chuck walked up to the car, standing slightly behind the driver's door, the rapist said "Good evening, officer." He then fired a single shot from a .357 derringer. The bullet struck Chuck in the throat, dropping him where he stood.

The rapist drove off into the night, assaulting the victim and driving from one small Texas town to another.

Chuck was paralyzed from the neck down; he lived, lying on his back in a hospital bed. He died from complications about a year later. He was given the hero's burial he deserved.

Almost twenty years later, after I had served as the Lieutenant of SWAT for three years and was now in charge of the communications center and a new information system my wife woke me to tell me that Keith Rodriguez had been killed on a SWAT mission.

The news and friends told this simple but awful story: While Keith was prying open the door of a drug dealer's mobile home, the drug dealer broke out the small window in the door and fired one shot that bypassed Keith's Threat Level III vest, severed his aorta, and killed him in about twenty seconds.

Keith was a Travis County success story. He had graduated from a local high school and eventually got a job working in the jail. He quickly gained self-esteem and a career path. He was promoted to Corrections Officer II, tested for and was accepted for patrol, worked in patrol till he was eligible to attend the sixty-hour basic SWAT school. Upon successful completion of the school, he applied to SWAT. He had now worked for the Travis County Sheriff's Office for over five years and he had found his calling.

I was the lieutenant of the team when Keith went through training and applied for SWAT. I was very selective about who was eligible for this team.

Not only would the candidate have to have the obvious characteristics of excellent strength, stamina, shooting skills and quick intelligence for rapid problem-solving, but, each candidate also had to pass an extensive background investigation. No history of citizen complaints was acceptable. No misunderstandings between co-workers, no record of injured suspects during the arrest.

We had to have strong and capable cops for SWAT, but we also had to have cops who were not "hair triggers" nor were likely to take a bad situation and make it worse.

We carefully and completely interviewed past supervisors and reviewed every arrest report involving the candidate for the years prior to their application.

Keith passed with flying colors.

A family man, he spent his off-duty time involved with his wife and sons. Coaching softball, attending church and making home repairs were the tasks he enjoyed.

On duty, he was a solid team member. He was always ready to do his job and ready to help his partner get his part done. He was ready and capable of taking on any task in the lineup of the entry team members.

Additionally, he cross-trained in counter-sniper operations to make him a well-rounded SWAT team member.

In January of 1996, he attended a military school put on by JTF6, for SWAT teams involved in counter-drug operations. It was called "Recondo training."

The Army had created the school in the sixties during Vietnam. It was a combination of the long-range reconnaissance school and the hard fighting commando training. Hence the name "Recondo."

It taught officers to survive in hostile places, to keep their heads and locate the target, make the mission be successful and get home.

In the 1965 school, the final exam put the student under live conditions, tracking enemies that were tracking him. Failure meant death. It was a serious hard-ass school.

In January 1996, it was nineteen degrees and sleeting. The class started on a Sunday afternoon and would not end until Saturday at noon. We soon learned the Army instructors were going to make this training be as serious as the original. Class days were twenty hours long. We had dorms on the military base, but we were locked out after the first day. No shelter, no food, no water. We were given instruction in winter survival techniques, so we built carefully camouflaged shelters, learned how to melt the ice from the tree branches for water and tracked mice for food.

All while being presented with "hunt and find the bad guys before they find and kill you" scenarios. At 2:00 am we would be carrying forty-five-pound packs quietly through the frozen forest, with no lights to guide us and making no sound as we moved, following specific compass headings for miles to locate the "target" before the "target" located us.

Once we located the target, we had to capture them. When we were done, we got to sleep for four hours in a camouflaged hole.

It was seven long cold days of intense hard fighting and difficult work. We came home from the Recondo training competent, strong and capable of long difficult missions.

Keith loved every minute of it.

He excelled at it. He was in his environment.

His loss will long be recognized as an awful occurrence.

Chapter Seven

Training to Triumph: From Classroom to Critical Incidents

I had the wonderful opportunity to work in the training academy on two separate occasions, once as an instructor and again as the lieutenant in charge of all training. I spent a total of six years with the academy.

Working in training really teaches you. You have to know the material to teach it, and there is nothing like a know-it-all, been-there-done-that, old-timer sitting in your classroom to keep you on your toes.

I taught Texas Penal Code, Intermediate Traffic Law and Defensive Tactics, the sort of stuff you would expect.

There are three types of training for cops.

First, basic training, called BPOC, for the Basic Peace Officer Course, over six hundred hours of state-defined courses that build a solid foundation. Some agencies incorporate their city codes and policies into this basic training. Some teach only what the state requires. For eight years we held the grant funding that provided this training to the ten-county area of Central Texas. I can travel anywhere in this eight-thousand-square-mile area and meet cops that I trained.

The next type is Field Training. This may be the most powerful. It is the pairing of a senior officer with an Academy graduate. Extensive studies have shown that the best officers to use for this sort of training are <u>not</u> the fifteen to twenty-year veterans. It is the younger, twenty-four to thirty-six-month member of the force who makes the best field training officer, called an FTO.

This guy or gal was still new enough to remember how it felt to learn the procedures and rules that the trainee was going through. While an old-timer might make fewer mistakes and be more certain of the correct answer, they often lack the answer to the question "Why?" The old-timer answer is too often, "Because, that's the way we do it." Or, "We have always done it like that."

While those answers give the old guy a feeling of time and consistency, it doesn't help the trainee associate the required task with the overall goals and missions of a law enforcement agency.

A new guy has to be able to understand the whole picture of why it is important to write a report a certain way, or why it is important to make a copy of the report for the prosecutor's office.

The third type of training is continuing education courses. There are changes to the laws, there are new investigative procedures, and there are skills that need to be honed. Constant training is necessary to maintain sharp cops.

I have been involved in all three of these and have enjoyed the benefits from all of them.

While assigned the job of Lieutenant of Training, I attended a week-long hostage negotiation school and then a sixty-hour SWAT school.

I applied for a position on the all-volunteer SWAT team and was accepted as both an entry team member and negotiator.

Today, a situation can occur where the "One Riot, One Ranger" philosophy just will not work.

A house load of brain-fried, drug-using, lab monkeys, heavily armed with the latest firearms is a good example.

Too often, in the quiet rural areas of our countryside, methamphetamine labs have sprouted. Out there in the woods, heavily armed extremely paranoid drug manufacturers are cooking illegal substances for users in the nearby cities.

These people are constantly in fear of being turned in by friends they have cheated or of being found out by the authorities, and because of their drug use they sleep very little. And because of the lack of sleep and drug use they become so paranoid that they will shoot first and ask questions later.

They are extremely volatile to deal with. They have been in jail before and do not want to go again. Going to jail means going "cold turkey" off their drug habit, a painful and emotionally damaging ordeal. Going to jail means a loss of their income and what little bit of house and home they have scratched out of their illicit dealings.

They shoot each other over the slightest issues. I know of at least one case where the victim arrived at the emergency room with an "accidental gunshot wound" that was really the result of an "OK Corral" sort of shootout between him and another drug dealer near Lake Travis.

A good SWAT team reduces the risk of injury to everyone, good guys and bad guys. By having highly trained personnel and well-planned missions, bad guys are often arrested without a single shot being fired.

Even though these people are very dangerous, with good intelligence about the layout of the house, the bad guy's habits, number and type of weapons and knowing exactly the correct time to break down the door, we could enter the location and have everyone under control in a matter of seconds.

We constantly practiced the basics of moving ten to twelve SWAT guys through doorways, through rooms, around corners, upstairs and in and out of deployment vans for hours on end. All so that we could seamlessly have fire-cover on every possible location as we moved to arrest the actors.

No careless muzzle sweeps were permitted. A muzzle sweep is when a cop moves his weapon from one target location to another and during the move accidentally points the weapon at a fellow officer, even for a fraction of a second. But a moving group will change target locations as they move through a warehouse, wooded area or a car dozens, sometimes hundreds of times. Consequently, we had to practice thoroughly to know where each member was and where each was going.

As a group, we learned each other's techniques and methods; we were highly aware of each other's movements and could perform each other's jobs with less than a second of notice.

These skills are so polished that they will perish without constant rehearsal and practice.

To maintain that level of proficiency, a person has to have a commitment to fitness, equipment maintenance, and skill rehearsals, and an ability to mentally focus on difficult and stressful tasks, even when cold, hungry, tired or injured.

We trained so that we were capable of handling any kind of threat.

We had extra tools. Automatic weapons, tear gas, smoke, ballistic shields, sophisticated optic and audio systems were all components we were competent at handling.

CS and CN gas have been around for years and could be effective in crowd control or encouraging persons to exit a structure. CS is an abbreviation for O-chlorobenzylidene malononitrile. The properties of this compound were first discovered by American chemists in 1928, and the potential chemical warfare uses were suggested by a Dutch writer in 1934. During World War Two scientists in various countries studied the effects of the compound but it wasn't seriously developed as a weapon until the mid 1950's. CN, or chloroacetophenone, was investigated but not used, during the First and Second World Wars, and was used by United States forces in Vietnam. As its toxicity is apparently greater than that of CS gas, it has largely been supplanted by CS gas. Like CS gas, this compound is irritating to the mucous membranes.

While on call for negotiation, I got a call from another agency about dawn one morning. A distraught young Hispanic man had had an argument with his wife, during which he shot some holes through the roof. The wife left and called the police. Now the young man had been holding off the DPS SWAT team all night. They had figured they would just wait him out, but after twelve hours they called for help. They wanted someone to talk him out.

I arrived and began to gather information about the young man and the situation.

I learned that the state team had fired tear gas into the three-bedroom house using twelve-gauge shotgun rounds about three hours into the situation and had decided the guy had a homemade gas mask; otherwise he would have come out.

I tried the phone, because they insisted on it. No one answered. After an hour I talked with their commander. I explained that this guy was Hispanic, he was male, he was young and he had had an argument with his wife. He has a pride that will not allow him to surrender. He could never surrender. He had to be persuaded. I suggested they insert gas again.

The commander reluctantly agreed.

I watched through binoculars as the team approached the house and shot one round of gas through a broken window.

"Gas is in," They radioed.

The commander looked at me, as if to say, "See, he isn't coming out."

I finally understood that they were doing what they were trained to do.

The team had trained in the insertion of gas and had always shot one round in practice. It was a cost-saving measure. Why use twelve or twenty rounds of gas just for practice? Most of the work to insert gas was getting the team in place. A safe slow method of moving within range was what they had long practiced. The only problem was the team thought one round was all that was ever needed.

This was a wood frame, claptrap, broken window, leaky roof, country farmhouse.

I knew from my early associations with Air Force EST teams that gas should pour out of the structure for it to be effective. I clearly recall gas training in the early eighties at Bergstrom Air Force Base; we had access to a cinderblock "house" used for fire training. With our instructor inside we had to shoot enough gas into the two-story structure (that had no coverings on its windows or doors) to convince the instructor to come out.

It would not happen with one round of gas. He wouldn't come out until there was so much gas that it appeared as heavy smoke in and out of the structure.

I told the DPS commander, "You have got to use more gas. Make it BOIL."

He radioed the commands to his team, and we began hearing numerous reports of the twelve-gauge rounds. "Keep it up," I said, looking at the house and still not seeing any gas vapors.

Finally, after about thirty rounds, the young man came running out the front door. Gas was pouring out the door behind him, flowing from his clothes and coming from his hair. He left a trail of wispy white smoky gas as he approached with his hands held high.

He needed a serious threat to provide him with the appropriate reason to surrender. He needed a lot of gas. He didn't need negotiation.

About 1990, we started working with OC spray. Oleoresin capsicum, is the refined burning component in hot peppers.

In some cases, tear gas was not effective, like with trained attack dogs. More and more, as police were making the approach on a dangerous drug dealer's location, one or more badly treated, extremely vicious dogs would confront the team right at the moment of entry.

SWAT teams all over the US have tried different tactics for handling dogs. Tear gas was quickly recognized as having no effect on an attacking dog. Sometimes a CO2 fire extinguisher could disorient and confuse a dog long enough for the team to get past him. And sometimes the CO2 had no effect at all. The fallback position was to shoot the dog.

We had missions where shooting the dog was necessary and no one liked it. It wasn't the dog's fault that he was trained to attack everyone who came to the house. But a dog could put the entire mission and therefore the lives of the entire team in jeopardy.

Ten seconds is a long time on a SWAT entry.

All a dog had to do was attack one team member and slow the entry by a few precious seconds. Those seconds would be plenty of time for a paranoid drug dealer to get his fully automatic machine gun and open fire on the team.

So when handheld OC spray became available we quickly got training in its use. We were interested in seeing if it was effective on dogs.

It didn't take long to find out.

One night our team got the call from the city's narcotic unit. The San Antonio narcs had located one of their drug dealers in South Austin. He was wanted for murder and drug dealing. He had been killing off his competition in San Antonio and had a reputation for a very short temper.

The narcs had the house staked out and were able to provide "eyes on" intelligence. One of their informants was sent to the door to ask about the truck in the front yard with a for-sale sign on it.

To everyone's delight, the target himself came to the door, walked outside for an excellent visual confirmation and showed the truck to the informant. The informant said that he was interested in buying and would be back later, hopefully ensuring that the target would stay put waiting for his return.

We had about an hour and a half from the time of notification until we needed to be on site.

We were briefed by both the San Antonio and Austin guys at the Austin narcotic office.

This guy was bad. A Hispanic man standing six foot three and weighing two hundred and sixty-five pounds, he was always armed. During our informant's visit, the target had a .45-caliber semi-automatic pistol in his pants. They told us that he was wanted for one murder in San Antonio, but was suspected in three others. He knew that the police were looking for him; that's why he was ninety miles from San Antonio, in Austin. He would be ready for a fight.

Rather than wait until dawn, when most folks are nicely asleep and much easier to take by surprise, it was decided we should go now, for no one knew where he would be by tomorrow. Unlike TV, tailing a suspect, without the suspect knowing, is very difficult and requires lots of folks in lots of different vehicles. A luxury we didn't have.

And there was a dog.

Not just any dog, but a large Rottweiler that tried to bite the informant when he came into the yard.

I got the job of taking care of the dog. I was given a canister of OC and as backup, a sawed-off, pistol-gripped twelve-gauge shotgun with a shoulder sling.

I could handle the OC in my left hand and have the shotgun in my right. The shoulder sling carried the weight of the gun on my right shoulder with the muzzle pointing downward. All I had to do was push down on the pistol grip and the shotgun muzzle would raise to a shooting position. It was pump action, so the first shot was going to have to be good.

As the team readied, I practiced my exit from the van with both hands occupied and practiced having the shotgun come up when I wanted it to.

I was going to be the first out of our van, with twelve other team members right on my heels.

We would travel in a straight line toward the entry point of the house. When I located the dog, I was to break away from the group, engage and contain the dog.

"Engage and contain." That meant, getting the dog to attack me, thus allowing the team to make a smooth entry. Then I was to do whatever was necessary to keep the dog from getting to me or other team members.

I have a close friend on the team, Jack, who would be the third person out of the van. He came up to me and asked me if I thought I could take care of the dog. "Sure, Jack" I told him, "If the OC doesn't work, I will shoot him."

"Well, just be sure, because it sounds like a bad dog." Jack responded.

I told him that it would work out, one way or the other.

I knew that Jack had a fear of dogs. He had told me of an off-duty encounter when he was "treed" up a street sign post by a pack of dogs one day while he was out for a training run. I tried to exude confidence that I could take care of the dog. But I could tell Jack was worried.

After a few more practices, we loaded the van, a plain, white, windowless delivery van and began the drive to the target location.

When we got a few minutes away, our team leader made radio contact with the narcs who were still sitting in the dark near the location.

They told us that the guy was still inside the house. Good news.

As we came around the next-to-last corner, our team leader told them we were less than a block away. The narcs excitedly radioed that the target had stepped out on the front porch.

Bad news. That meant he would be aware of our approach.

"Continue to the target," came the calm command from our guy.

"The target is on the front porch and I can see the gun in his waistband," radioed the narc.

I couldn't see anything. I could just feel the van slow rapidly and know that the target would be on the same side as the door and the rest of the team would exit.

There were about half a dozen narcotics guys in various cars around the site, all watching as we exploded out of the van.

I came out fast and focused on finding the dog.

There he was, sitting on the porch right next to the drug dealer. OC spray in one hand and the shotgun, barrel up, in the other, even as I rapidly crossed the yard, I could see the gun in the guy's belt line.

Because we approached in a straight line, the dog initially saw us as one object (and a bad guy had only one target to shoot at). I made eye contact with the dog and moved to my left.

Recalling this incident, it seems like a long time passed, in slow motion. But it only took a few seconds.

These images are burnt into my memory.

The dog and I made eye contact.

I moved forward and to the left, to make me different from the group.

The dog and I maintained our mutual confrontational stare.

He dropped his shoulders and came off the porch.

He was big, going over one hundred and ten pounds.

He was on target for me. We are on a collision course with each other.

I needed him on me and away from the team.

I knew that I had moved about four feet to the left of the team, giving them a clear shot at the bad guy and thus able to take care of business.

The dog didn't growl, bark, or make any sound, he was just coming hard and fast. Mouth open, ears back, shoulders down, teeth bared.

He ran to meet me at full speed.

I had the shotgun barrel up and my finger just outside the trigger guard.

As the dog got close, I gave him a shot of the new OC spray straight into his eyes and mouth. He kept coming.

I gave him another blast; I had decided that when he was close enough to put the barrel in his mouth, only then would I pull the trigger.

In the corner of my vision, I was only vaguely aware that the bad guy had voluntarily taken a face dive onto the porch. He was lying face down and had given up.

As I gave the dog a third blast of spray, I watched his mouth come within an inch of the barrel, I was about to pull the trigger when the dog snapped his eyes and mouth shut, turned and ran away!

The spray finally took effect.

I looked over at the bad guy and saw Jack finishing putting the handcuffs on this asshole.

An easy arrest, that's always a good thing.

The dog retreated to the far side of the yard and didn't return.

Soon enough, the bad guy is placed in the back of a waiting patrol car.

The mission is successful and complete.

I noticed that the narcotic guys were very happy, jocular even, laughing and slapping Jack on the back.

My team members were also laughing. "That was great!" one tells Jack.

"Jack has come up with a new technique to capture bad guys!" They laughed.

"His way, they will always give up!" another chimes.

Another giggles.

"Really, how's that?" I ask.

"Didn't you hear him?" asked a team member, "Didn't you hear Jack?"

No, I admit that I didn't hear anything.

"He was yelling at you, Tommy."

Concerned about the dog, he was yelling, loud enough for all the other cops and the bad guy to hear: "Shoot him, Tommy! Shoot him, Tommy! Shoot that son of bitch, NOW!"

Chapter Eight

The Art of Speed, Surprise, and Violence

Back in those days, one of our primary techniques was called "Speed, Surprise and Violence of Action". Today's SWAT teams work differently from how we did then and for their safety I am not going to publicly discuss today's tactics. But that "Speed, Surprise and Violence of Action" was a very useful tool for many teams. It meant that we were focused on highly dynamic actions with the intent to overwhelm and capture or cease the movement of any bad guys.

We approached a threat in a straight line, thereby presenting the smallest target possible. All team members' weapons were pointed at the threat, thereby bringing the maximum firepower to bear, if necessary. Each team member had a specific duty and job for each mission. The first in the line was in charge of Breech or entry. He usually carried a ram or pry tool so that he could quickly open the door or window and then step out of the way to allow the full team to enter. The next in line was "Point" or Number One, since he or she would be the first through the entrance. The Point is intent on locating the most dangerous target inside the building. The number two person is the "Alternate Point" and takes any alternate route that Number One does not take. Number Three is the number one guy's partner and moves in a two-man formation to locate bad guys with number one. Number Four is the partner to number two and moves with him as they take a different direction inside the building. The number five guy takes a different direction than either number one or number two and his partner is the number seven person in the lineup. This continues until all team members are inside the building. This alternating partnership allows for very fast movement through doorways and quickly floods a house or business with two-man teams on the hunt for the bad guys. All team members were required to know what each other's job or assignment was and be able to fill that assignment at any time.

On one occasion I was number three and knew that I was to accompany the number one guy to the most probable location of the bad guys. We had been briefed by the local narcotics team that they had arrest and search warrants for a local auto repair shop. The main bad guy was going to be in an office just on the other side of the reception area. Our approach went fine. The van came to a stop, the doors popped open and we began the rapid orderly exit. Most of us did, that is. The Point man somehow got his pant leg wedged in the hinge of the van door. When he got up to get out, he fell on the ground and under the rear bumper. The "ram man" moved to the door. The Point was still under the bumper as the entire rest of the team stacked and staged. The ram swung back and then into the door, Boom! The Number two was now number one and I was now number two. The entire lineup's responsibilities had now changed. In less than a second, everyone had new jobs. There was no time to discuss it, no time to make verbal cues, no time to do anything but "dynamically" change the plan and continue with the job we were there to do. I knew the man in front of me was now going to move quickly through the reception area heading for the internal office. My job was now to take another direction of travel and locate and eliminate any threat in that area. My view of the reception area was blocked by the team member in front of me as we moved quickly through the doorway. As soon as I cleared the door, I turned hard left, as the internal office was straight ahead. Immediately across the room from me was the man sitting behind a desk. He was facing me. "Police!" I yelled. "Down! Face down!" I ordered, as I closed the distance between us. He placed his palms on the desk and pushed himself back and raised his hands a few inches from the desktop. I was now all the way across the room and could see the butt of a pistol in his waistband. His reluctance to get down, or to raise his hands over his head coupled with the weapon in his waistband must have accelerated my actions. I needed to get control of him quickly or shoot him before he pulled that gun out of his pants. The desk was between us. In less than a second, I was going to have this guy in custody or I was going to have to shoot him. Our training teaches us to keep our trigger finger outside the trigger guard until the moment of trigger pull. That turned out to be a good thing. Without slowing down from the breakneck speed that I had entered the room, I came straight over the top of the desk and pool-cued the muzzle of my MP-5 nine-millimeter submachine gun exactly between his eyes. My defense tactics (CQB) training had taught me to maintain direct eye contact with my adversary while being hyper-aware of his hand and foot movements. I was locked in a death stare as I launched across the desk. "Down, Face Down!", I repeated. The muzzle hit him with all my weight and my velocity. He went down. Face down. I recovered the .357 magnum from his waistband and was pleased to see my partner leaning in to place handcuffs on the now docile bad guy. Moments later, the "All clear" was shouted and we knew all the bad guys were in handcuffs. My partner looked at our suspect and then at me and smiled a huge smile. He said, "What were you trying to do? Give him a tattoo?" I looked at the suspect and to my surprise, he had a perfect MP-5 muzzle-shaped strawberry between his eyes! Our training had paid off. Another bad guy in custody without a shot fired. Without the repetitious training that we endured, the team would have been endangered if we had to take the time to regroup after Mike's pants got stuck and he fell under the van. In those few seconds, the guy behind the desk would have heard the discussion and the approach and then pulled that gun from his pants and fired when we came through the door. Without that training I might have followed the "new" number one in and missed the bad guy to the left, giving him a few moments to pull that gun. And without our training, I would have had my finger on the trigger and my fully automatic Heckler Kock MP-5 nine-millimeter submachine gun's trigger would have been squeezed when I struck him and I would have blown that guy to kingdom come.

For local teams like ours, those calls of dangerous drug dealers made up over half the calls we got.

We also got "barricaded subject" situations that were most often "distraught husband" calls. Sometimes they went into a true hostage situation.

About once a month, some man (usually married, white and middle-aged) would crack under the pressure of his sub-standard life.

He would fire some shots through the ceiling, scare all the other family members out of the house, then threaten suicide for hours while our team waited outside.

These types of calls were recognized as a negotiation job, but you had to have the team in place. The team insured the subject remained at that location, and narrowed his options to talking with the negotiator.

Without a team, these guys would get in a car and drive to a friend or other family member's house.

That meant putting someone else at risk. A suicidal subject does not have any regard for anyone else's life when he is ready to take his own. So, allowing him to travel somewhere and get someone else involved is very risky.

By studying past similar incidents from around the US, we learned some fairly consistent factors.

First, the longer the negotiations took, the more likely we would get a peaceful resolution.

The longer it took, the more likely the emotional high would wear off and we could have a reasonable conversation.

The longer it took, the more the alcohol or other drugs would wear off, allowing more rational thinking.

The longer it took, the more the hostage taker and the hostage would bond, in a condition named the Stockholm Syndrome. The Stockholm Syndrome is named after the city in Sweden where it was first documented and studied.

A bank robbery went bad and the robbers took hostages. It was learned that the hostages and hostage-takers developed dependent relationships.

In extreme situations this relationship can be a bad thing and probably caused Patricia Hurst who had been kidnapped (in the sixties) and held in captivity by her captors for months to believe that she should assist her captors. She then was an active participant in a bank robbery with this group.

But in a surrounded house or bank, it was a good thing. Bad-tempered bank robbers were less likely to injure or kill a hostage with whom they had developed a relationship.

In the fifteen years I was involved as our primary negotiator, the only downside to an extended situation was the "we need to do something" feeling that many folks get.

It could affect anyone near the scene. Neighbors, friends, media, the big brass, and anyone who was watching the events unfold.

It is a natural reaction. Almost every human being will experience this feeling. "We need to do something."

In many critical situations, doing something often means survival.

If you are watching a building burn or a boat sinking, that feeling gets you motivated and into action. Action can save lives and property.

But in a barricaded or hostage situation, doing something means taking some action, which all too often forces the bad guy into a reaction that can kill or injure others.

What must be kept in mind in these extended situations is that the bad guy has taken this action out of deep desperation. He lacks control of his life and has taken this desperate action in a last-ditch effort to gain control.

If he feels that the cops are attempting to take control of him, he will react.

He feels like he has no other choices. His situation didn't come up just today; he has had these awful that he lacked control of his life for a long time.

Maybe his boss is always on his ass at work, and when he gets home, his spouse is indifferent to his problems. Then some checks bounce, and after a few weeks, he still cannot make his boss happy and his wife is still a bitch.

The guy has blown up and shot out the lights because he desires control of his life and this is the only thing he thinks he can do to regain control.

It is our job to get him to see that there are other avenues and that killing himself and others is not the only thing he can do to retain control.

But if the SWAT team does something during this time, it challenges him for control of the situation. And he is in a frame of mind that tells him that he will do anything, including killing loved ones, to hold on to what little control he has.

During these situations, people can get the perception that nothing is being done. When a high-ranking police official takes stock of a situation he may realize that we have twelve SWAT guys surrounding the house, the neighbors have been removed from their homes to prevent the bad guy from accidentally shooting through their houses and the streets are blocked so that other folks cannot get to their homes and this situation has been going on for hours. Additionally, we haven't been constantly on the phone with the guy and then the media arrives, sets up cameras and they and others will begin asking the head cop, "What are you doing to resolve this awful situation?" "When will this be over?" "How long will you allow this to go on?"

The top cop feels the pressure and asks the SWAT commander in charge, "What are you doing to resolve this awful situation?"

We would politely explain to the new sheriff or captain that these things took time. Right now, no one is getting hurt and we have the situation controlled to prevent anyone else from getting hurt. We had the guy "contained" and that meant that eventually we would talk and with good negotiation skills, we would talk the guy into giving up.

It always took a while.

Years ago, when I was the on-call negotiator and entry team member, we had an incident with a drunk biker who had found out that his mother-in-law had changed her will to leave the house he lived in from his wife to a different daughter.

This thug was an out-of-work welder, whose truck had broken down, his wife couldn't/wouldn't hold a job, and they had to live with her mother, a stroke victim who was confined to a wheelchair. They were so poor, that when light bulbs burnt out, they didn't get replaced, and when the air conditioner quit that summer, they didn't get it fixed. In Texas, that is unheard of.

That hot summer night, after having a few beers, he discovered the truth about his mother-in-law's will and it really pissed him off.

He got his .44 magnum pistol from the bedroom and began firing in the house. The wife and children ran to the neighbor's house. The mother-in-law, stuck in her wheelchair, didn't escape.

While the wife was calling 9-1-1 from next door, he was taking his frustrations out on this poor old lady. Beating her with the pistol and berating her with verbal abuse to assuage his wounded ego.

Patrol responded and quickly called for SWAT. Fearing for the life of the old woman, the SWAT team gingerly entered the house.

The bad guy had barricaded himself and the old lady in a bathroom, located in the center of the house. It had only one door and no windows.

The team members said while they could hear him cursing and beating her, they could also hear her weak cries for help.

Stacked and ready for an entry, just outside the bathroom, one of the team members brushed against the wall and the guy heard them.

He yelled that if it was police, they should get out, and then he began firing that .44 through the wall. One bullet struck the back of a grandfather clock next to a team member's head.

They backed out of the house.

As difficult as that was, that was the correct thing to do.

They had heard the woman's cries. That meant that she was alive.

A forced entry at that point would have forced the bad guy to take the only action he could. He would shoot the woman as the team broke down the bathroom door.

They had to leave. They had to back off.

It was difficult to do.

But it was the right thing to do. They saved that woman's life by doing that.

I arrived about five minutes after the last shots had been fired, got briefed by the commander and approached the front door.

On the front sidewalk, just outside the house, I was stationed behind a small ballistic shield with a bullhorn.

This asshole wouldn't allow us to insert a throw phone, nor would he leave the bathroom to answer the phone in the living room. I settled down on the cool concrete and began talking.

Open-ended questions, non-accusatory statements and a relaxed, "we can work this out" attitude are the opening tools for a negotiator.

"Tell me what happened" are often magic words.

This asshole, who is seconds away from killing his mother-in-law and himself, hears that someone is interested in his side of the story.

Someone wants him to explain how it got this way. It may be the first time in days that he has gotten to speak openly and freely, telling all his woes and troubles. Getting to tell his story without interruption or contradiction from a nagging wife or witchy old mother-in-law.

It begins the connection.

We talked into the night. We talked about motorcycles and guns. We discussed politics and women. There was no rush. I was there to learn about him and understand him. He had an audience that would listen. After four hours, the beer was wearing off and he began to lose his gusto.

We talked about what it would be like if he were to just give up.

He had seen too many movies and TV shows, where the bad guy walks out of the house and the cops gun him down. He wanted to give up, but he was certain that we would gun him down as soon as he was outside.

I told him that was the sixties, that we were in the eighties now and that we didn't do things like that. I tried to make him understand that he was dealing with a different sort of law enforcement agency.

He wouldn't budge.

What could I do to assure him that we were not going to kill him when he came outside?

Finally, he decided that if his lawyer were outside with us, he would know for sure that we wouldn't kill him and that he would come out. He says that he and his lawyer have a drunk beer and shotguns together, they are buddies and that he wants him to be outside.

Another thing we learned from reviewing hostage and barricade incidents from around the country was to be very careful about requests to bring specific persons to the scene for the bad guy to talk with.

If a subject refuses to talk with the police negotiator but says that he will discuss the situation with a family member or friend, then the subject may be planning an "I told you so" suicide. What he wanted was to cause the person the maximum amount of pain, in retribution for the pain they had caused him.

He would make all the appearances of giving up, of being willing to talk to a friend, or family member, even come outside (for everyone to see) and then he would blow his brains out, causing everyone huge emotional trauma. Or even worse, he would shoot the family member, only to be gunned down by the police seconds too late.

Only in rare and controlled situations would we allow family or friends to be involved in negotiations.

Even if the intent wasn't for an "I told you so" suicide, they were not trained in negotiations and could innocently cause the negotiations to take a bad turn.

For example, by agreeing with the bad guy in an effort to show sympathy, a person might agree that "this situation was the worst thing that had ever happened."

If the bad guy believes that, then the next logical assumption is that there is no way to correct the situation, that it has gone too far to be able to get back into anything normal, and he might as well begin shooting everybody and everything. It can go bad real quick, if the wrong words are said.

Such a statement would be negated by a trained negotiator. No matter how bad it was, the negotiator would tell the bad guy, "It's not so bad that we can't work it out."

By leaving that small door open to resolution, the trained negotiator knows how to guide the thinking of the bad guy to eventually get him to come outside, with his hands up, and to lie face down in the yard.

So bringing an unknown person to the scene was risky.

Risky to the situation, even risky to the person.

We discussed the idea at some length before we decided to bring the lawyer to the command post, about a block from the house, and talk with him to see if he would cooperate.

We found his phone number by tiptoeing into the master bedroom and looking it up on the suspect's home computer -- a computer that wasn't running Windows and would today be a real antique.

Back at the command post, I called the attorney and told him what was going on. He was cooperative and understanding on the phone.

I then explained that the bad guy had said that he would give up if the attorney was in the front yard with the police, and he agreed to come to the scene.

During the forty-five minutes it took for the lawyer to drive to our location, I talked to the bad guy and told him that his attorney friend was on the way and told him what we wanted in terms of a surrender plan.

A surrender plan is a must. There can be no surprises and no assumptions at that point. When the SWAT guys are ready for the suspect to "trick" them and when the bad guy thinks that the police just want a clear view so they can shoot him, you have to have a preplanned choreography of events.

I told the guy he had to leave his weapons in the house, walk out the front door with both hands held high, stop on the sidewalk and follow the police instructions. He would be handcuffed and searched.

The instruction he would receive would be to stop, turn all the way around (this would allow us to see if he had any bulges of hidden weapons in his clothing), then face forward, kneel down, and finally lay face down. He would be instructed to turn his head away from the approaching arrest team. He does not need to know how many they are or see them approach.

Constantly covered by our snipers with their high-powered .308-caliber rifles, this guy's head would explode if he pulled a gun from his shirt or if he tried to grab a gun from the approaching arrest team.

I didn't tell him those things. Some things are better left unsaid.

The arrest team would be three SWAT guys, two to do the work while the other provided close-range firearms coverage.

We constantly trained in CQB, "close quarter battle." We were good at it. But in a one-on-one situation, bad things can happen very quickly. Fractions of seconds define life and death. A skilled CQB fighter can disarm his adversary and shoot him with his own gun in less than a heartbeat.

We took no chances. The three-man arrest team would be armed with HK MP5 fully automatic nine-millimeter machine guns. These guns were loaded with thirty rounds, so if this guy tried to do anything but follow our exact surrender instructions, he would be a hair's width away from death.

The attorney arrived and approached the command post. I had given him exact driving instructions that would bring him into the subdivision and directly to the first checkpoint of the outer perimeter.

The outer perimeter was several city blocks in size. It was the zone in which we had evacuated nearby residents to prevent them from being an accidental victim. No one but police and authorized personnel were allowed inside. Marked patrol units manned by uniformed officers stood vigilant against any intrusion. In the past, we had bad guys call for reinforcements from their friends, who would then drive to the scene, only to be stopped by the uniformed cops.

The attorney was properly escorted by a uniformed officer directly to me. He made introductions and I told the officer, in the presence of the attorney, that I was now responsible for his actions and would take any action necessary to control him or prevent any criminal incident.

I looked at the attorney and explained. "We are inside the security of the outer perimeter, and you and I will soon enter the next level of security, the inner perimeter. No one but SWAT and negotiators go inside that circle. Except for tonight. Tonight, if you are willing to follow my every command, I will take you inside that very serious and dangerous area. Your friend has been drinking and has fired shots at his wife and at our SWAT guys. Just because you and he have a relationship does not mean that he will not harm you. He is in a very paranoid state, where he believes the police will kill him if he comes outside. He is not unlike a trapped wild animal. His behavior is very unpredictable. He may think that you are part of some plot to kill him. You and I will be protected by our approach and a small ballistic shield. You will have to do exactly what I tell you. If, for any reason, you do not obey my instructions, I will assume that you are attempting a criminal act and I will do whatever it takes to effectively cease your movements and remove you from the area. Do you agree to follow my instructions?"

His eyes had not left mine as I spoke. He swallowed and nodded his head and said "Yes."

I knew that I had his attention; I also knew that he was scared.

I told him to follow me; I instructed the SWAT commander to notify the troops that we were coming in and prepare for the surrender process.

We walked away from the lights of the command post, into the dark of the night. When we got one block from the house, I whispered to him that we would crawl from here.

We got on all fours and crawled towards the house. When we were two hundred feet away, I pushed him down into a belly crawl and said to stay below the curb line to avoid gunfire from the house.

He followed me down the street, then onto the sidewalk and up to the ballistic shield, waiting for us.

The shield is not wide enough for us to lie side by side and be safely behind it. I put him squarely behind it and lay on top of him.

This is a good position for me. I can control him if I need to and I can whisper instructions easily into his ear.

He followed my instructions and picked up the bullhorn, saying the exact words that I would say into his ear. "Charlie, it's me, Bob Snickle. I'm here in the front yard with the police; I will make sure they do not hurt you."

Sure enough, after a few minutes, Charlie responded and surrendered without incident.

I let the attorney get up and greet Charlie, and then escorted him outside the outer perimeter as his friend was placed in the backseat of the waiting squad car.

Not all such incidents go that smoothly. Sometimes the crook does things that require you to go outside the regular planned routines.

It was Super Bowl Sunday, 1995, about 11:00 am when we got the call.

I was now the lieutenant of the SWAT team and was the first person dispatch called when a woman had dialed 9-1-1 to say that her ex-boyfriend may have just shot himself and now wouldn't answer the phone.

She had been talking to this alcoholic scum on the phone as he pleaded with her to reconsider and come back to him. When she said that she would not come back, he told her that he was going to kill himself. She still said she would not return (smart girl) and she heard what sounded like a gunshot, and then the phone fell to the floor followed by no response from him.

She tried calling back a few times, and then called 9-1-1 (instead of driving out to his lake house, which is what he wanted her to do. Again, smart girl). Nine-One-One notified EMS, who stated they would respond but would not approach any closer than half a mile until police had entered and determined the scene was safe for paramedics.

Marked units responded and set up a perimeter around the remote lake house. They called for SWAT.

The first thing to do even before arriving at the scene is to assign a "react team" of SWAT guys. Generally, three to five guys, armed with handguns, gas and MP5s, would be placed near the situation, radioing to me any movements or occurrences from the incident location.

A react team was immediately "eyes on" for a SWAT commander. While I was still driving to the scene, I would be in radio contact with them. They would provide a picture of exactly what was going on. And if the circumstances indicated that the bad guy was killing or severely injuring people now, then I could give the command for them to enter and take action.

In 1983, James Oliver Huberty killed twenty-one people in a McDonald's as SWAT guys, waiting outside, followed the SWAT commander's orders not to shoot or enter the restaurant until he got to the scene.

That type of tragedy did not need to be repeated.

This day, I arrived about the same time the react team was getting stationed.

The house was located at the end of a tree-lined curving dirt driveway. No other houses were nearby. The react team had a clear view of the front of the house. They radioed that they saw no movement.

Due to the distance from the hospital, the county medical helicopter had arrived at the scene, and seeing an opportunity to get a new and eager sheriff out of my hair, I suggested that he ride in the helicopter to gain an overall view of the situation and provide us with situational reconnaissance.

I was assuming the helicopter pilot would maintain a certain safe distance from the house, based on the pilot's medical training and desire to prevent injury.

I was wrong.

The pilot was a Vietnam vet and was unafraid of a few handgun rounds. When the Sheriff asked him to get closer, he took him right in.

The circling helicopter attracted the attention of our suspect, who was quite healthy, sitting in his house, having another beer in preparation for the big game.

When he stepped outside the front door to better see the helicopter, my reaction team informed me of his every move.

"Lew, he is on the front porch, facing the AB corner, looking up, watching the helicopter."

"Lew" is short for lieutenant. The AB corner would be the front left corner of the house. I knew the team was near the AD corner, the front right corner of the house.

"The helicopter is circling very low. He is lighting a cigarette," they continued.

"Take him," I said. "Take him, now."

I knew several things: the noise from the helicopter would cover the sound of these four guys approaching. The asshole was facing up and away from their approach. His attention was significantly distracted.

Because they could see him lighting a cigarette, I knew they could see his hands, and because they didn't say anything about a gun in one of his hands, I knew the weapon wasn't immediately available.

Additionally, I could be reasonably sure that he was our bad guy, as the ex-girlfriend had told us that he lived alone and had no friends.

And finally, I was confident of our guys. Not only did we run ten to fifteen miles every week for stamina, but we ran sprints for speed. One member had been a player on a semiprofessional soccer team. He would be in front and would be very fast. The others would be right on his tail. When we ran twenty-yard sprints, we all finished within one second of each other.

I was fifty yards away when I gave the order. I ran toward the house, watching their bullet-like approach.

Four SWAT guys running in a straight line, one behind the other, weighing a total of six hundred and fifty pounds, hit this guy in the back without him ever knowing they were coming.

They drove him to the ground.

I got by their side, as they moved into their cuffing routine. He was face down with two holding him down, one holding him at gunpoint and one placing handcuffs on him.

I bent down and removed the burning cigarette that lay on the driveway next to his face.

What a total loser.

Super Bowl Sunday, woods full of SWAT guys, helicopters flying around his house, EMS paramedics pulling into the driveway to check him for injuries, with four cops still on his back, he looks up at me and asks,

"Is this about those parking tickets?"

Chapter Nine

The Making of a SWAT Team

Needless to say, a SWAT team has to be in great physical condition.

We had to be strong, that was obvious, so we could break doors and take down bad guys. But we also needed stamina. We needed to be able to wear forty to fifty pounds of gear, in the hot Texas sun, for hours, and for that we needed super endurance.

We had the good fortune to have mandatory fitness testing for all staff begin in 1989. This meant by 1993, when I was the lieutenant of the unit, we all had been participating in the required annual fitness testing for four years had been involved in a regular workout program and had received training in fitness and diet.

We ran, lifted weights and ate healthy foods. We were in great shape.

To get the best training, we went to the Institute for Aerobic Research in Dallas, founded in 1970 by Dr. Kenneth Cooper. This is the guy who invented the word "Aerobic." He has built an extensive research facility to determine what fitness is and how it affects mortality. There we got certified as fitness specialists and learned the aerobic exercises, the muscle-building activities and the healthy eating habits necessary to build really fit cops.

Our fitness testing was based on the standards established by the Institute.

Dr. Cooper's Institute had tested tens of thousands of people of all fitness levels of all ages and both sexes. The results are that "fitness" is a very definite and measurable condition. By testing a person's stamina, strength, flexibility and overall body condition, a measurement of fitness can be determined.

In 1989 the required fitness level of the team was set at the sixty-percentile level. That meant that 40% of the population could attain those marks.

In 1993, I raised the required fitness level to the eighty-percentile level -- meaning that only 20% of the population would be able to attain those measurements –- and we tested every three months.

The tests consisted of running a mile and a half in a very short time, lifting weights, doing sit-ups, measuring flexibility and body fat.

After the first full year of quarterly testing, our tests showed that we were in the 90-95% percentile. We were running fast, lifting heavy and carrying no extra fat.

This team was in incredible shape. Because this level of fitness came about gradually, we were not aware of just how fit we were.

We had gradually grown used to the gnawing feeling each day that if we didn't have an early morning mission, or early long run or workout, by 10:00 am our bodies began to desire exercise.

At that level, your body would ache for exercise. We had to get some kind of workout in, every day.

We had also gradually grown used to the eating machines that we had become. That level of fitness meant that our bodies were akin to highly tuned race cars. We needed fuel, the highest quality and lots of it.

Marv Souza, one of our SWAT guys, laughingly told the story of when he was asked not to come back to the all-you-can-eat buffet at a local New York deli-style restaurant.

Darold and Dave learned how fast they were one day. They were at a probation office to arrest a violator when the offender decided to run.

He had a ten-yard head start on Darold and was headed for a glass door out of the building. From a dead stop, Darold caught him in less than half the distance. Regrettably, the bad guy went through the glass of the door as Darold tackled him. I suggested that next time he let him get outside. They realized that they could allow a runner to get outside and they would still be fast enough to catch him.

Other realizations about just how fit we were came about. Roger McMann commented that during a foot pursuit, he was able to talk to his partner while chasing down a fleet-footed felon. "I think we should wait till he crosses that grassy area ahead to take him down."

The city narcotic guys found out about our quickness and developed a "buy/bust" methodology for cutting down on crack sales near schools. The narcs would cruise into a neighborhood in a tricked-out sports van and sell crack cocaine to the addicts that flagged them down, only to have a couple of our team members jump out of the van upon the completion of the sale and chase them down.

None of the city narcs had the speed to run down a whacked-out crackhead.

Our guys loved the exercise and the narcs loved the arrest statistics.

When not training for SWAT missions, or involved in SWAT missions, we hunted the felons who had active arrest warrants.

One day when I was working in the office, as a lieutenant does sometimes, I got a call from a man asking who was going to pay for the damage to his vehicle. He said one of my team members had jumped on the roof of his car.

Jumped on his roof?

I asked him for a bit more detail and he explained that two of my team members had given him my name and number to call as they were taking someone to jail.

I asked him to tell me what he knew, got his name and telephone number and told him that I would call him back.

I needed more information.

I needed to hear from my guys.

It didn't take long; they called once they got to the booking desk.

Darold and Eva were hunting a bad guy in an apartment complex. They had a new address for this turd on the second floor of the complex. While knocking on the door of the corner apartment, Darold said that he heard a window open around the other side; they both checked and saw their quarry running away from them at full speed. He was headed for the end of the exterior walkway, where someone had removed the protective railing.

Eva ran to go get the car as Darold committed to the foot pursuit. Being partners, they knew how to divide and conquer.

When the bad guy got to the end of the walkway, he ran right off the edge of the second floor and landed on the roof of a car parked below in the parking lot. Darold never slowed down.

He followed this wacko foot and step, through a twenty-foot leap with a vertical drop of twelve feet, landing on the same car and sprinting off down the parking lot.

Eva blocked the other exit and Darold captured the would-be escapee in the parking lot. They fought for a minute till they had the cuffs on him and put him in their car.

That is when the owner of the car approached and asked them who was going to pay for the damage to his car.

Without hesitation, they gave out my name and number and left for the jail.

On the other end of the phone, I closed my eyes and shook my head.

"Darold, are you okay? Did you twist a knee or anything in that landing?"

"I'm fine L.T. He had already mashed in the roof, so it was a soft landing."

I was smiling, still shaking my head.

I took it as part of my job as the lieutenant; I called the citizen back to help him work with his insurance company to get his car repaired.

Besides being able to run like the wind and stand ready to enter a hostile situation all day long, we were strong.

Strength is a necessary requirement; an example is opening the door of a mobile home.

Unlike most residential doors, mobile home doors open outwards. This means that the "usual" method of opening a locked door by hitting it with a fifty-pound ram on the locking device will not open such a door.

Even a one-hundred-pound weakling can swing a ram at a conventional door, and if he hits the knob or lock, the physics of the ram will open the door.

Opening a metal mobile home that moves <u>outward</u>, was another trick.

We found a positive method for opening mobile home doors was to to hit the door in the center, hard enough to fold it. That took strength.

One dawn raid, after opening the door in such a manner, we found the drug dealer's girlfriend had been standing behind the door when we hit it. She was knocked fifteen feet across the room and was sitting on the floor against the opposite wall when we entered. She was okay, but very stunned.

A highly trained team is always ready and always prepared. The bad guys are not always the ones to make things get crazy.

One fine spring morning, a father and son were opening their sign-making shop in the eastern part of Travis County. It was just after 9:00 am when an armed robber came into their store. A cokehead is in need of a fix. He pointed a semiautomatic handgun at the son and demanded the money.

The victim was cool and honest. This was a sign shop, he said. They didn't have a cash register, and they didn't get a lot of walk-in traffic. They hadn't been to the bank that morning and didn't have cash on hand.

Angered, the cokehead demanded to search the rest of the store. In the back, they met up with the father. Again, the robber demanded money. As before, both the father and son were straightforward and honest with the nutcase robber.

They didn't have any money; they emptied their pockets and offered the robber about twenty dollars.

The father engaged the robber in a concerned conversation. By asking, "What has happened that makes you so desperate? You seem like a regular guy. What has happened?"

The robber told a big fat lie and said his mother was in the hospital and he needed the money for an operation she required.

The father offered that he would go to the bank and get the robber some money. They decided on three hundred dollars. The father and son then asked the robber if he wanted to wait and the robber realized he was at risk of being seen and reported by a passerby. So, he said he was leaving and would come back.

"How will you know when I am back from the bank?" asked the father.

The robber gave him his pager number and said that he should page him when he wanted him to come back.

The robber left, the father and son called 9-1-1 and the Sheriff's Office sent a marked unit to investigate the incident.

After a few minutes of interviewing this highly resourceful and intelligent father and son team, the deputy got to the part about the robber giving his pager number to be notified when to return.

Thinking the robber probably would not return, the deputy instructed the father to call the pager. The robber called back and to everyone's surprise, he said that he would return in one hour to pick up his money.

They smiled at each other for a minute and then realized the danger.

The armed robber was returning to discover that he had been duped. He would not be a happy camper when confronted by the lone patrolman. Each had a gun. The likelihood of someone getting hurt was very high.

The patrol guy called for SWAT.

Dispatch got me on the phone and filled me in.

Holy shit! We had to act and act fast.

I grabbed the hippie van and had dispatch notify the team to meet me on a side street about two miles from the incident location.

The hippie van is an old-style "Good Times" van. Multicolored, smoked-out windows with a jacked-up rear end. Inside, it had a driver and copilot seat and nothing else except shag carpet on the floor, the walls and ceiling.

It was a good surveillance vehicle and sometimes we used it for SWAT deployments.

The team met with me and assignments were given out.

We arrived at the incident location and began preparations.

We quickly relocated everyone in the strip shopping center to one store in the far corner.

We re-parked all the cars in front of the store, leaving only one space empty.

We then loaded ourselves into the hippie van and backed across the street into another parking lot.

Our plan was this: When the robber returned, he would have only that empty spot to park in. The victims provided us with an excellent vehicle description. He would be driving a late 1980's model blue Chevrolet pickup with a license plate that started with TCG.

When he pulled into the empty space, I would stack the hippie van on his rear bumper and maintain close contact to prevent him from being able to move his truck.

The team would exit the van and form into two groups, one for either side of the target truck. He would be presented with an obvious situation in which surrender would be his best choice

Each side had security, distraction devices, tools and gas.

A distraction device is a class C explosive. It is designed to make a very bright flash and a loud bang to distract the attention of a bad guy and give the tactical team a few extra seconds to get control of him.

It has no projectiles and causes no damage if a person is more than twelve inches away from it. It can get hot and cause a burn, but only if it comes in contact with combustible materials. Mostly, it is a very loud bang and the very bright flash of light.

The sound level at discharge is one hundred and seventy-five decibels; the light level is 2,550,000 candelas. The duration of the explosion is ten milliseconds. It has a half-second delay on the activator.

Most often referred to as a "flash bang," these tools provide that extra time for a team to enter the house, or would distract the bad guys from being able to get to their weapons before SWAT guys were on top of them and could put handcuffs on them.

We were in a position with no time to spare.

About two minutes passed and here came the truck. He pulled into the empty space and I put the van smack on his bumper. I gassed it a bit and could feel his front tires contact the curb.

The teams exited the van and approached, one on each side of the truck.

Five SWAT guys on each side, fully automatic weapons pointing at him. What else would he do, but give up?

"Hands!" the team leader shouted.

The robber looked right at him. Then he turned his head and looked at the other team.

"Hands!" The order was given again.

He looked back at the first team.

Lying on the seat beside him was his semiautomatic handgun.

He looked down at the gun. Back up at the team.

"Hands! Show me your hands!"

He turned and looked at the other team.

This idiot was going to pick up his gun!

If he did that, we were going to have to shoot him before he shot one of us.

Before he could pick up the gun, the team leader, Rick tapped the break-and-rake guy.

Entry team members had different jobs and carried different tools. One team member would carry a crow bar to break glass to facilitate the entry of the team or a flashbang.

That tap readied the flash-bang operator. Darold broke the window of the truck and less than a second later, Dave placed the flash bang inside the truck.

BOOM!

All the windows expanded and spider webbed.

The robber fell limp behind the steering wheel.

He looked dead.

He was removed from the truck and our tactical paramedic quickly triaged him.

He was unconscious, but okay.

Our team trained and worked tightly together. They were ready and capable of any problem. Instead of waiting until this guy had stepped over a line that he would never return from (picking up the gun on the front seat), this team had effectively apprehended the bad guy and had even saved his life.

I was a very proud SWAT lieutenant that day.

He remained semiconscious while being transported to the ER.

His mother wasn't in the hospital and he later claimed that he had no memory of the robbery whatsoever.

He was convicted and sentenced to ten years.

Chapter Ten

The Cost of Surprise: From Caballo Negro to Waco

There is a SWAT mission that most people in the nation are familiar with. It happened at the end of February 1993.

Things went real bad, real fast.

There are things that I saw and heard that day that are engraved in my memory, the sights and sounds that scar emotions and last a lifetime.

None of us who were there would ever be the same.

A significant tactic designed to maintain the element of surprise used during that mission had its roots in a separate SWAT mission in October of the previous year.

We were at Camp Swift, a military base forty-five minutes east of Austin, training for a mission.

Op Sec was being strictly enforced. "Op Sec," short for operations security, referred to the fact that details of an upcoming mission were known only to those who actually needed to know them.

We were not told the location of the mission. Any names or descriptions of suspects would not be revealed; even the date and nature of the mission would be kept secret until the final briefing, just minutes before the actual raid.

We were practicing riding in and exiting a cattle trailer. Once we arrived at the target location (drawn on the ground at Camp Swift with crime scene tape) we would exit the trailer and quickly move to our assigned positions and perform our required duties.

There were fourteen of us in the trailer. I was in one of two "break and rake" teams. My team was to break a window, and then remove any blinds, drapes or other blocking materials to facilitate an easy entry.

In this case, entry was not by a person or team but a distraction device, (like the one used on the robber who came back for his money in Chapter Nine).

There were three of us on each team. I had a crowbar with which to break and rake, another team member had a distraction device to be placed inside the window after raking, and the last team member had security for the other two. Security means that he would have his weapon out and pointed at the window to protect us while our hands were occupied performing other tasks and not able to defend ourselves if a lethal threat were presented against us.

The other eight members of the team would breach the door between the two windows and enter the structure.

It seemed simple enough, but riding in a cattle trailer didn't make sense, until the morning of the raid.

The morning of the raid we were paged at 2:00 am and instructed to meet at a recently closed air force base in one hour for the briefing.

When we arrived, we were shown in a large auditorium. On stage was a representative from the federal agency, Drug Enforcement Agency (DEA).

The place was packed. I looked around and estimated two hundred and fifty cops. When the briefing began, the DEA guy told us it was three hundred cops.

He talked for thirty minutes, explaining that a multi-agency task force had been working on this drug operation for the past eighteen months. They had learned the drug dealers were bringing in ten kilos of black tar heroin from Mexico each week. The kingpin of the operation was a Hispanic woman who lived on a quarterhorse ranch east of town. She used the ranch as the initial dropoff and then had the drugs and money moved through twelve other businesses located in and around Austin.

Because the street name for black tar heroin was "black horse," this mission was given the Spanish name -- Caballo Negro.

The DEA agent said the SWAT team (that was us) would take the main target and her staff. The rest of the two hundred and eighty-six officers would simultaneously hit the other businesses and homes of the other conspirators.

We were told the woman had become very paranoid and had been telling the informant that she knew the Feds were coming for her, and when they did it was going to be a blood bath. She showed the informant fully automatic weapons and told him that she kept them in bed with her. She was ready for a fight.

We were told that she slept with either her boyfriend in one bedroom of the mobile home or in the other bedroom with her bodyguard.

It now became clear why there were two break-and-rake teams and why we were traveling in a cattle trailer.

Because it was October and cool outside, the cattle trailer had wooden boards between the metal rails, supposedly to help keep the cattle or horses warm. It provided a bit of concealment, but it was still a cold ride out to the ranch.

As we turned off the paved road and onto the dirt road leading to the ranch house, we crossed an old, rickety cattle guard. It clanged loudly as the truck crossed, and then again when the trailer crossed.

We were told during the briefing that this was their early warning system. Whenever anyone drove in, it acted like a doorbell and announced an arrival.

They now knew we were coming.

We still had a long quarter-mile drive to the house.

As we pulled to a stop in front of the house, the sun was just breaking the horizon, carefully timed; we would have light to operate by.

We quickly approached our positions; my instructions were not to break the window until the door ram hit the front door. We wanted strict noise control until the moment of entry.

I stood poised with my crowbar cocked over my right shoulder in a batting stance. I was expected to hit a home run that morning. The window was to my left; I was facing the eight-man team and was waiting and watching as the ram man approached the door.

In the corner of my vision, to the left, I saw movement in the window. I knew it was our target.

Our security man was Jack.

Rick held the flashbang.

Jack was yelling, "There she is! There she is!"

I saw that he was locked in a stare with the woman. I knew that my life and Rick's life were in his hands. If she or her boyfriend brought a gun muzzle to bear on us, Jack would "take out the threat."

I would not be able to respond with my weapon. I was waiting to see the ram swing.

Just as I was sure that she was going to open fire and Jack was going to have to return fire, with my head less than a foot from the window, the ram began to swing. I timed my movement with his.

As he hit the door, my crowbar was breaking through the window.

Just before impact with the glass, I saw her face disappear and the blinds snap back into place.

I crashed the crowbar through the window, then swung it in a large circle inside the window, then gave the handle a spin and drug out the blinds and shades. In less than 2 seconds the window was now very open.

Rick deftly dropped the flash-bang inside the window and into the bed with the two criminals.

BOOM! Our bang went off.

BOOM! The other team's bang went off.

The house rocked on its foundation from the hit on the door and eight SWAT guys entered in a rapid single file.

We later reviewed the videotape. From the time the ram hit the front door until the team members inside had handcuffs on the crazy drug-dealing woman and her boyfriend, it was seven seconds.

That's both fast and slow. Fast to break a door and find and handcuff someone. Slow, in that seven seconds gives someone a long time to decide whether or not to shoot.

It was obvious that our strategy to arrive in a cattle trailer gave us a few extra precious seconds. Without those extra seconds, we would have been involved in a confrontation with gun-toting paranoid drug dealers. The conclusion of that confrontation was sure to leave someone or several others injured or dead. Everyone agreed that it was a good idea to bring the team on-site in the cattle trailer. It confused the target and her cohorts long enough for us to get into place and drop flash bangs in bed with them. The entry team reported that the woman and her boyfriend were rolling off the bed in a dazed state as they came into the bedroom.

The rest of the raids all went just as flawlessly. No problems. Pounds of drugs and thousands of dollars were seized. All the bad guys were arrested. A very successful mission.

Four months later, on February 28th at 9:20am, our pagers went off, again.

It was a cold, drizzly Sunday morning.

"Hostage situation, north, stage at the Seventh Street office." That's what the decoded pager message said.

When we met, our Chief Deputy of Law Enforcement was present. His brother, an Alcohol, Tobacco and Firearms (ATF) agent, had called him. ATF was involved in a mission that had gone bad and they needed our help, now. They were asking for a rescue from the unexpected ambush they were trapped in.

No one knew the exact causalities, but we were told there had been serious injuries to the ATF guys.

We loaded four Crown Victorias with all our gear and four SWAT guys in each and headed for Waco.

One hundred miles north of Austin on IH 35, it took us less than an hour to get there.

My mouth is dry and my fingers are cold as I begin to write what happened next.

We drove outside of Waco down a small country road. Ambulances, police cars and helicopters seemed to be scattered around the fields and roadways.

When we stopped, we were met by a tearful ATF agent who hugged our team leaders and cried for a few minutes, before explaining they had a truce with the Davidians. There would be no rescue. They had negotiated a cease-fire. We were needed for containment, now.

I had never seen such a distinguished and mature man exhibit such raw emotion. Dressed in blue ATF BDUs, tears ran down his face and he began telling our team leaders how he and the other ATF agents found themselves in an ambush.

It was extremely painful to watch him explain how the ATF had called Koresh and asked for the cease-fire to rescue their injured and remove their dead agents from the compound. The cease fire was finally agreed upon and he pulled back and called for ambulances and medical assistance.

As he told his painful story, I was looking at the wet grass at my feet and realized that it was stained dark red -- shiny and red. In a mashed-down spot. My gaze rose a bit and I realized I was looking at a discarded threat level III ballistic vest. It was open and lying in the grass.

At first it didn't make any sense to me. Why would anyone leave such an expensive and necessary item lying out here in this field?

Then the combination of the mashed-down grass, the slick greasy dark-red fluid and the other pieces of SWAT gear (a helmet, gloves and eye protection), told me that I was standing in a triage area.

Not long ago, bleeding and dying police officers were here.

I heard the ATF agent say that he knew three agents had been killed. Later we would learn that four had been killed and sixteen injured. There would be no rescue.

I looked up at the large wooden and rambling compound and could see armed snipers looking at me through telescopic sights. We were standing in the shadow of hell. All the while, the ATF agent talked on.

We were in the middle of a killing field. And this man was asking for our help.

Many of you watched the failed raid on CNN; we did not see the news until almost thirty hours later.

Doing what a SWAT team is designed to do, we took up positions to contain the situation and facilitate negotiations.

I was assigned to a sniper/observation team directly in front of the compound.

We monitored all movements and coordinated the release of dozens of women and children that night from the Davidian compound.

We were to rotate duties, but no one could sleep. We kept our eyes on the compound for the next twenty hours.

By 9:00 am the next morning the FBI had enough staff on site to take over all perimeter duties.

We were debriefed and sent home.

Only after returning to our homes and loved ones did we see the news.

Only then did we see the cattle trailers pulled by pickup trucks abandoned in front of the Mount Carmel compound and realize the element of surprise that worked for Caballo Negro did not work here.

Chapter Eleven

The Tac Medic Evolution

In 1994 we became aware of a gap in our problem resolution plans. That was the response time of trained paramedics to an incident location with SWAT in the remote parts of the county. Due to ambulance coverage plans, we could not always request having Advanced Life Support personnel accompany us to a few blocks from the scene and then be in "stand by" mode for several hours. Travis County is over 900 square miles and our EMS is a combined Austin-Travis County EMS. They had to be staffed to handle the denser populated city of Austin and have staffing that could respond anywhere in the rural parts of the county. And drug labs and crazy people seem to like the rural parts. So, we had to wait until either we or the suspect or victim suffered an injury (which could be very life-threatening) before we could call for EMS support. Out in some parts of the county the response time would be very long. We needed this response time to be much shorter. I had been approached by paramedics of our well-respected local EMS agency. Some of them (as a result of their off-duty Army Reserve activities) had attended a superb school called CONTOMS. Standing for Counter Narcotics and Terrorism Operational Medical Support. This course taught them tactical techniques like how to triage a victim that they could neither see nor hear, as in a hostage situation and the only contact is through the hostage taker. They learned techniques for providing survivability without outside support from nearby hospitals, necessary when attending to injured personnel and in some of the remote areas we worked. They also had attained training in the importance of quiet and stealth movement, even when carrying lots of additional gear.

Out of the need for expert treatment, a short response time and involvement in dangerous situations, the concept of a cross-trained paramedic/ SWAT guy was born. We called the position the Tac Medic.

The requisites for involvement with the program were

1. Employed as a licensed paramedic practicing Advanced Life Support in the field.
2. Successful completion of the 60-hour Basic SWAT course, with the exception of the firearms training.
3. Eight hours or more per month of training with the SWAT team.
4. Quarterly Fitness testing at the 80% level, with 90-95% in at least two of the five tests.

Out of many that made applications for these positions we had only five that passed all the tests.

Joe Torres, Mike Kane, Elizabeth Payne, Jim Allday and Brian Griswold.

These brave team members carried an extra pager to be on call for our team. They worked their "usual" 40 hours a week and then responded to our calls for help, too.

They carried no firearms, they entered the danger zones and fields of fire with our team, carrying only their medic bag of supplies and their faith in our ability to defend them from hostile fire. We always did.

I am still amazed at their dedication and professionalism to have volunteered for such risk, under such difficult circumstances, with such high and stringent application procedures.

These dedicated individuals accompanied us on raids of drug labs, all night-long stakeouts and stressful dignitary protection missions. All without a firearm to protect themselves. They came with us to provide us the critical first aid during those crucial few seconds should one of us ever be injured.

Over the next few years, lucky for us, those life-saving services were never needed. But they accompanied our SWAT team on every mission, from drug raids, to plain clothes dignitary protection of District Judges, emergency responses to "man with a gun" calls and all those late-night barricaded subject calls. Always providing valuable strategic advice while planning each mission and providing immediate aid for the few minor injuries that bad guys sometimes get during an arrest.

I thank these folks every day for their unselfish devotion to that incredibly difficult job they performed.

Chapter Twelve

The Foundations of Effective Policing

We all want the same thing from our police officers, regardless of who we are—rich or poor, black or white, young or old. What we ask for isn't complicated: we want officers who do the right thing. Officers who don't bend or break the law, but can still handle the worst criminals. Conservatives, liberals—it doesn't matter where you stand politically; we can all agree on this. We want law enforcement that acts appropriately, using the right judgment at the right time.

At its core, law enforcement has two primary goals: preventing crime and apprehending criminals. Neither is easy, and both require careful action. Let's start with crime prevention. We know 100% prevention is impossible. To even come close, we'd need a cop for every citizen, which would be wildly expensive and incredibly invasive. But what we can expect is a visible police presence in public places to deter crime. We want officers who are alert and watchful, who keep an eye out for threats to our children and our property.

Then there's catching criminals. It's not just about the arrest; it's about gathering solid, reliable evidence that will hold up in court. We expect law enforcement to do more than just nab the bad guy. We want them to build a strong case, preserving evidence that ensures the criminal is convicted and sentenced appropriately.

This balance between prevention and apprehension relies on appropriate actions. We don't want officers going behind our backs with wiretaps or secret investigations unless there's a real, pressing need. But when they do make an arrest, we want it done right—by the book. This expectation has deep roots. Since the founding of this country, we've demanded that law enforcement act reasonably. That's why the Constitution says, in essence, "No arrest without a warrant." If someone's going to be arrested, there needs to be documented, reasonable evidence presented to a judge. It's a system that ensures fairness and prevents abuse of power.

But what counts as "appropriate action" changes with time and place. Back in the 1800s, a sheriff was expected to chase down a criminal, face him in a shootout, and come out on top. That was seen as appropriate law enforcement back then. Today, things are different. Our communities are bigger, and we don't know everyone the way we used to. So now, we rely on clear, convincing evidence before declaring someone guilty. We need warrants, arrests, and prosecutions that are thorough and well-documented so that when a jury says, "Yes, that person is guilty," we're sure they've got the right person.

Our understanding of what's appropriate has shifted over the years, but the principle remains the same. We want officers to act appropriately. What's acceptable in New York may not be the same as what's acceptable in Austin, but in both places, people expect their police to act with integrity.

Consider the Rodney King case. We all saw the video footage, and for most of us, it was clear that what happened wasn't right. Yet in the first trial, the officers were acquitted. How could that be? The defense managed to convince a jury that the police officers had acted appropriately. They pointed out that the California Highway Patrol had initiated the chase, and when Rodney King finally stopped, the Los

Angeles police stepped in. The Highway Patrol officers only had firearms, but the LAPD had less-lethal options: a stun gun and batons.

Before the camera started rolling, Rodney King had ignored police commands and charged at the officers. Sergeant Koon used a stun gun on him twice, but King kept getting back up. When the camera started recording, we saw King charging at Officer Powell, who reacted by swinging his baton. What most people didn't know at the time was that crucial seconds of the video were edited out before the footage was shown to the world. Once the jury saw the full, unedited version, they were swayed. They understood that, in their view, the officers had saved King's life that night by using non-lethal force.

Yet even with that context, the public outcry was intense. People saw the tape and felt that the officers had gone too far. Even though the LAPD didn't shoot King, the repeated baton strikes felt like excessive force. Why? Because as a society, we expect officers to have better options. And when we see something that feels wrong, we speak out.

But how do officers know what's appropriate in any given situation? It starts with good people and solid training. But there's something important to consider about police training. In the academy, recruits spend hours on nightstick techniques, even more time on firearms training, but only a handful of hours on verbal conflict resolution. What tool do you think officers will fall back on in a crisis? It's human nature to rely on what we know best when things get intense. In the case of the LAPD, the officers didn't have training in hand-to-hand combat techniques, so they used what they knew—batons and stun guns.

And that's where the problem lies. We need our police to be trained in a variety of conflict-resolution methods, so they have more options when things go wrong. They should know when to de-escalate verbally, when to use less-lethal force, and, only when necessary, when to use deadly force. With the right training, officers will be better prepared to make the right choices.

But training isn't enough. Officers need to be in tune with the communities they serve. They can't stay isolated, only interacting with other officers. If they do, they risk becoming detached from the concerns of the people they protect. Officers need to spend time in the community, not just on duty, but off duty as well. They need to be part of the neighborhood—attending local events, volunteering, and being visible in everyday life. When officers know their community, they're more likely to act in ways that align with what that community sees as appropriate.

Now, let's talk about the bigger picture. Most cops are doing the right thing. Day in and day out, they make the right decisions under incredibly tough circumstances. For every bad cop that makes headlines, there are thousands of good cops who quietly do their job the right way. Just look at the numbers. Take Austin, Texas, for example. Between the Sheriff's Office, the Austin Police Department, and the surrounding areas, there are around four thousand officers. Every day, each of these officers makes decisions about what to do in difficult situations. And overwhelmingly, they make the right call.

Yes, bad cops exist. And no one wants them gone more than the good cops do. Bad cops tarnish the badge, they damage the community's trust, and they make the job harder for everyone. But the solution is to get involved. Don't accept bad cops as inevitable. Ask questions, get to know your police, and be part of the conversation. This is the United States, and we don't have to accept bad policing as a way of life.

Remember, most officers are good. They're out there every day, working hard to keep us safe, making the right choices, and taking appropriate action. Let's give them the support they deserve, while holding the bad ones accountable. After all, we all want the same thing—cops who do the right thing.

Chapter Thirteen

Under the Beacon: A Night of Courage

Years ago, I told these stories to my daughter, with parental editing, at bedtime.

Later when she was a college student and after her first review of the draft of this book, she said that I had left out one of her favorites.

So here it is.

For my daughter, Kari.

Told in bedtime-story style.

Once upon a time, there was a very bad man. His name was Richard Ahair. He was a chronic alcoholic and had a mean streak. He had a girlfriend, Sheila Brown, who thought she loved him.

Richard beat up Sheila almost every day. He hit her with his fists. He would get drunk and get mad and hit Sheila for no reason at all. He told her that she deserved it. Sheila tried to help Richard, but finally one day she realized that he was never going to change.

She left him.

Things were fine for a few weeks. Then one day while she was eating dinner at a restaurant with some friends Richard drove by and saw her car in the restaurant parking lot.

Her friends later told me that Sheila was sitting with her back at the door, so she never saw Richard walking in. He didn't say a word, he walked up behind her and grabbed her by the ponytail, flashed a hunting knife at the others, and dragged Sheila backward out of her chair, across the floor and out the door. The last they saw of her, Richard was dragging her across the parking lot. Sheila was screaming for help. Her friends were worried for Sheila's life.

They called 9-1-1.

As luck would have it, I was less than a minute away when the call came out on the radio. I pulled into the parking lot, got the story from her friends and asked which way Richard had taken Sheila. They pointed into the dark, down a long row of parked cars.

I took my flashlight in my left hand and my service revolver in my right hand. I had learned not to hold the light in front of me, identifying my exact location. I held the powerful light up and to the left above my left shoulder. I wanted the illumination but I knew the light could make a target of me.

It didn't take long to find them. I could hear Sheila crying for help and Richard cursing and hitting her.

I quickly shined my powerful flashlight on Richard and said, "Sheriff's Office, drop the knife!"

Richard looked right at me and cursed. He didn't drop the knife.

As I repeated my order for him to drop the knife, he cursed and stabbed the knife in my direction.

I noticed that he wasn't looking at me, but directly into the beam of my flashlight. I moved closer, getting inside his lunge distance.

He was trying to look mean and confident, but he was mistaken about my location.

I was invisible to him. To him, I was the bright light. The bright light of authority that he had spent all his years in defiance of, I thought to myself. He would face the light and curse for all he was worth.

It gave me an idea.

While keeping the flashlight in the same place, I moved my body to my left, holstered my gun, took control of the light with my right hand, and kept moving forward and left. All the while keeping the light in the exact same place.

Now, instead of being in front of Richard, where he continued to wetly sputter obscenities and hatred, I was beside him, next to his outstretched right hand that held the knife.

While he was occupied shouting at my light, I took his knife hand in my left and performed a wrist-lock take-down.

This quickly opens the attacker's hand, forces the knife to drop free and allows me to drive the attacker to the ground, face down, easy for handcuffing. I executed the maneuver and it worked perfectly.

I quickly placed the handcuffs on him and escorted him to my patrol car.

Richard was taken to jail and sentenced to five years in the penitentiary.

Sheila and her friends were very relieved.

A few months later, Sheila met someone nice who didn't have drug or alcohol problems and they lived happily ever after.

Good night, darling daughter.

Sleep tight.

Tommy Blackwell lives in Travis County with his wife, Carol.

Printed in Great Britain
by Amazon

59440453R00096